42 Rules of Marketing

by Laura Lowell

E-mail: info@superstarpress.com
20660 Stevens Creek Blvd., Suite 210
Cupertino, CA 95014

First Printing: September 2007
Paperback ISBN: 0-9799428-0-2 (978-0-9799428-0-8)
Place of Publication: Silicon Valley, California, USA
Library of Congress Number: 2007936178

eBook ISBN: 0-9799428-1-0 (978-0-9799428-1-5)

Trademarks

All terms mentioned in this book that are known to be trademarks or service marks have been appropriately capitalized. Super Star Press™ cannot attest to the accuracy of this information. Use of a term in this book should not be regarded as affecting the validity of any trademark or service mark.

Warning and Disclaimer

This book is designed to provide insight and commentary on marketing principles and practices. You are urged to read available material, learn as much as possible about marketing, and tailor the information to your individual needs. For more information, see the many resources in the section titled "Interesting things to read and do." You can always visit the website at www.42rules.com.

Every effort has been made to make this book as complete and as accurate as possible, but no warranty of fitness is implied. The information provided is on an "as is" basis. The author and the publisher shall have neither liability nor responsibility to any person or entity with respect to an loss or damages arising from the information contained in this book.

If you do not wish to be bound by the above, you may return this book to the publisher for a full refund.

Praise For This Book!

"These 42 Rules are gems of advice and gentle reminders that every marketer needs to hear from time to time, packaged in concise, fun-to-read nuggets. If "marketing" is in your title, you need to have this book in your library."

Chris Shipley, Co-Founder, Guidewire Group Inc.
Executive Producer of the DEMO Conference

"Laura's insights in The 42 Rules of Marketing are invaluable. The book is an easy and fun read, and is a great reminder of many of the things that we marketers know intuitively but may have forgotten in the rush of doing our daily jobs."

Brian Lawley, President, 280 Group, and
Silicon Valley Product Management Association

"This book is full of practical reminders that help marketers stay focused on what works."

Karilee Wirthlin, Founder and Managing Principal, KL Consulting
President, Women in Consulting

"It's an actionable guide for anyone looking to improve the quality of their marketing. Laura's rules have sparked ideas with me and my team and have helped us make a lot of progress. Keep it on your desk, refer to it often and tell a friend."

Melissa Johnson, Director, Annual Fund, Walter A. Haas School of Business, UC Berkeley

"It's a funny, honest look at how marketing really works. Laura has written a book that captures the basics we know about but don't always do."

Kathy Johnson, Co-Founder, Consort Partners

Publisher

- Mitchell Levy, http://www.happyabout.info/

Cover Designer

- Cate Calson, http://www.calsongraphics.com/

Copy Editor

- Suhag Shirodkar, http://www.teclarity.com/

"You can have brilliant ideas, but if you can't get them across, your ideas won't get you anywhere."

Lee Iacocca
Chairman, Chrysler Corporation

Dedication

To Mom and Dad for teaching me to assume I can do anything.

To Rick for patience, support and unwavering enthusiasm for my tangents.

To Taylor and Riley for thinking it's cool.

Acknowledgements

Scores of people contributed to this book. It would be impossible to name and acknowledge everyone I've worked with over the years - all of whom have shared their experiences and insights with me, and indirectly influenced my perceptions of marketing.

I do want to thank some people who have directly contributed to this book. Without their input, the book would not be what it is.

To Valerie Romley for holding me accountable to myself and my vision; Kelli Glass for being my editor and having the patience to correct the same mistakes over and over again; Landon Ray for having the respect to ask me what I was really trying to do and inspiring me to do it.

In addition, the following people provided support, stories, feedback and motivation I counted on when I ran out of steam: Amy Bowers, Sally Thornton, Karla Carlen, Mike Freier, Walt Duflock, Hilary Glann, Jean Shimoguchi, Stacy McCarthy, Laura Thurman, Siobhan O'Connor, Jan McDaniel, and my sister and friend Pamela Castellanos.

Contents

Why 42? The concept of 42 rules is that almost anything in life can be summarized into 42 distinct ideas that capture the essence of the topic.

I am often asked "Why 42?" In the science-fiction novel turned cult film, *'The Hitchhikers Guide to the Galaxy'*, a computer is built to answer the "ultimate question of life, the universe, and everything." The answer is simply "42." As I approached writing this book, 27 rules seemed too low, but 51 were way too many. Douglas Adams, the author of The Hitchhikers Guide, was on to something when he chose 42. It felt right to me as well.

The *'42 Rules of Marketing'* is a compilation of ideas, theories, and practical approaches I have been collecting over the years. The idea was to create a series of helpful reminders; things that marketers know we should do, but don't always have the time or patience to do.

As you read through the rules, I ask that you don't take them literally. They are interesting stories, anecdotes and observations. Keep the book on your desk as it is intended as an "entertaining antidote" to long, boring conference calls. Don't read the rules in order, but flip through them until something strikes you. If it sparks an idea, then I've done what I set out to do.

Feel free to pass the rules along to anyone you think might benefit from a friendly little reminder. Use them to start a discussion about what other people think the rules should be. After all, these are my rules. What are yours?

1 Rules are Meant to be Broken

2 Marketing Must Result in Sales

Marketing is the way you create and distribute messages to get people's attention so you can convince them to buy more of your stuff

Marketing is creative, exciting and dare-I-say fun. Brainstorming ideas late into the night while munching on M&Ms and stale Doritos - what could be better? Throwing ideas around, watching them get better and bigger by the minute - how cool is that? Seeing your ad in print for the first time, or watching the results of an email campaign right after you hit the send button - it is pure adrenaline.

There was a time when brilliant creative was appreciated for being brilliant creative. Now, most CEOs actually want their marketing teams to help sell products. They are holding CMOs accountable for specific performance metrics - like all the other C-level folks at the table.

Marketing folks are, for the most part, not too fond of process, reporting or anything that might limit creativity. At least that's how most non-marketers view marketing people. Some marketers would certainly classify themselves as "right-brain" types, not inclined to documentation, data or discipline. Not everyone fits this description, and it might be hard for some of you to hear. Marketing is one of the last disciplines to apply process, automation and technology to improve both efficiency and effectiveness.

Speaking of effectiveness, what does it mean for a marketing campaign to be effective? Countless "people-years" have gone into trying to answer this question. Everything from click-through rates to brand awareness, net impressions and conversion rates can be used to measure the effectiveness of a campaign.

When you dig a little deeper, things get much simpler. At the end of the day, after all the creative is reviewed and approved, the copy is tweaked and refined, and the lists are scrubbed and de-duped, what really matters is that the campaign helped the company sell more products. Yep - it's that simple.

In the simplest terms, marketing is the way messages about your company, product or service are created and communicated to your customers in order to elicit a positive response. In other words, marketing is the way you create and distribute messages to get people's attention so you can convince them to buy more of your stuff.

The difficulty lies in directly connecting your marketing activities to increased sales. PR, for example, helps increase overall awareness of a company or product. Specific PR tactics like product reviews can even help position a specific product competitively and increase demand for the product. Think about the impact a positive review from Walt Mossberg of the Wall Street Journal has on a new technology product. Most people would agree that a positive review from Mr. Mossberg dramatically increases initial demand for a product. Nonetheless, it is still hard to directly link PR results to increased sales.

But at the same time, it is easy to directly connect other marketing activities to increased sales. Email and direct mail with a specific call-to-action phone number or URL can be tracked directly.

Don't over-analyze the point here. Marketing needs to help sell products. Yes, it is difficult. That's why they pay us the big bucks.

3 Plan a Little So You Can Do a Lot More

You need both Planners and Doers in order to get things done

After much observation and questioning, I have come to classify marketing people into two groups: Planners and Doers. This may seem a stereotype, and it probably is, but bear with me. Most people I talk to can definitely place themselves into either one camp or the other.

The Planners: You know these folks. They are endearing for their need to always "have a plan." They think, analyze, request more data and then reassess their assessment. Then something changes - ugh! After a moment of panic and deep breathing, they get to work. They go back to the plan and test their assumptions, review their contingencies and are quite proud to report that the plan is still workable "with a few tweaks."

These folks plan and plan and plan but actually don't do very much. Planners are important and we need them. Without them the Doers would be running around like chickens with their heads cut off! Remember the hit series Friends? The character Monica, played by Courtney Cox, was the epitome of a Planner. She had her life planned out from the time she was 12 years old. Not only did she plan her life, but her friends' lives as well. Everyone loved Monica because she was practical and you could always count on her to "have a plan."

The Doers: These folks, on the other hand, must be doing something. Anything. It doesn't matter what they do as long as they are "moving the needle" and "making progress." They have great ideas, and are excited and energetic. They are generally fun to be around. Because of the infectious spirit of the Doers, others jump on the bandwagon and everyone starts doing things.

The issue is whether the Doers are doing the right things. Are they consistent with the strategy and business objectives? Are they integrating with other activities going on? Are their activities repeatable? Can they grow over time? Back to the Friends example - Phoebe, as opposed to Monica was the quintessential Doer. She did whatever came to mind, whenever it came to mind. Everyone loved Phoebe because she was spontaneous and full of energy.

The point is, you need both Planners and Doers in order to get things done. Not everyone can walk the tightrope between planning and doing. And that's the biggest issue - the lack of balance between strategy and tactics.

Thanks to the Planners, companies can develop brilliant strategies - on paper at least. Thanks to the Doers, companies can spend a lot of time and money without much to show for it. What the lucky ones quickly learn is that developing a strategy is very different from executing one.

When companies try to implement their strategies, they run into obstacles such as channels, partners, technology, infrastructure, competition, or lack of resources. The reverse is also true. Companies can spend so much time executing that they lose sight of the business objective. For example, they might end up with an awesome website, but no incremental sales (see Rule 2.) To be valuable, strategy must be practical, and tactics must be integrated.

Planners and Doers tend to have difficulty connecting the dots between their plans (strategies, objectives, etc.) and their actions (tactics or activities). Lots of time, resources and money get wasted. This is a luxury of days gone by and one that business today can't afford.

My Mom used to tell me "if you slow down, you'll go faster" and she was right. How many times do you wish you'd just taken a minute to think something through before you jumped in? How about you? Are you a planner or a doer or maybe a little of both?

4 Know What You're Aiming At

Specific marketing tactics are the stepping-stones that ultimately get you to your vision

Before you start any marketing project, one of the first questions you need to ask is "What are our goals? What are we trying to accomplish?" Some people think this question is too basic. So it goes unasked, and unfortunately, unanswered. Without a clear answer, how do you know what to do? How do you know if you've been successful? How do you know if it worked?

According to Ken Jones, COO of Five Across, Inc. (acquired by Cisco and now a part of the Cisco Media Solutions Group), marketing strategy connects where you are today with your vision of where you want to be. Specific marketing tactics are the stepping stones that ultimately get you to your vision.

If your business objective is to build awareness for a new product line, you might have a marketing strategy to use partner relationships to increase awareness. If, however, your objective is to drive profitable growth, you might build an ongoing email campaign targeting existing customers. You might also develop efficient sales tools to support the high-growth markets, balancing growth and cost. Both approaches are credible ways of achieving the vision of profitable growth.

How can you choose between the two approaches if you don't have a clear understanding of what you're trying to accomplish? Without knowing your goals, you have no basis to evaluate your options. That means you can't make decisions effectively. On top of that, you can't evaluate the results of your project - because it isn't clear what you were trying to accomplish in the first place.

If you don't know what the objectives are, ask. If the objectives are unclear, ask for clarification. If there is disagreement over what the objectives are, ask someone to set the team straight "for the record."

Business objectives provide direction for your marketing strategies and plans. Business objectives can range from revenue, to market share to profitability and the list goes on. Marketing objectives can range from awareness (ensuring that your customers know you exist), to demand generation (attracting customers to your product), and lead conversion (converting prospects to revenue).

Awareness strategies make you more visible to your target customers. Quite simply, if potential customers do not know about a company, they will not purchase from it. In other words, you need to make sure customers and potential customers know you exist, and how you are better than their other alternatives.

Demand generation is exactly what it sounds like - the act of building demand for your products or services based on customer awareness, benefits and differentiation. Demand generation strategies and tactics attract customers so they can be converted into real customers who are willing to pay you money for your products or services.

This leads us to lead conversion. This is where the clicks turn into customers. This is when you finally get the purchase order signed after months of negotiating. This is when the customer says "I'll take it." This is when all your hard work finally pays off and someone buys your stuff

---

Awareness = Eyes and Ears
Demand Generation = Call, Click or Visit
Lead Conversion = Paying Customers

Rule

5 Pick the Problem You Want to Solve

People have opinions. Sometimes you agree with them and sometimes you don't. And sometimes you don't get to vote

The problem most companies have is that they have more ideas than they have resources (money or people) to implement them. You can't solve everything all at once, so you have to pick the problem you want to solve today. There will always be problems to solve. The important thing is to know what the problems are. Then you can prioritize which to tackle first and which to put off until next quarter (or the following quarter, or the next year...).

Prioritizing activities is difficult for most marketers because it means that something won't get done. By your very nature, you want to do everything you can to make your company or your product successful. The hard, cold fact is there usually isn't enough time, money or people to do everything you want to do - right now.

To get beyond this sometimes emotional reaction, ask yourself or your organization a very simple question; "If you can only do one thing - what would it be?"

The answer is your priority. It sets the context for evaluating other options. Which option helps you reach the objective...

- Faster?
- For less money?
- With better results?

Prioritization doesn't have to be complicated and doesn't have to take a lot of time. Try following these simple steps next time you're faced with a difficult prioritization challenge.

- Brainstorm a list of everything you'd like to accomplish in order to achieve your objectives.
- Outline the potential impact of each activity on the business objective.
- Estimate the cost of each activity (time, money and resources).
- Evaluate the likelihood of success.
- Identify the activities that provide the biggest return on investment (ROI).
- Prioritize the activities according to their ROI.

Armed with this information, you are better prepared for the inevitable budget discussions. Depending on the available budget, there is a point at which you will probably run out of money. By evaluating the ROI for each activity, you can determine how far your budget will actually take you. At this point, draw a line. The activities that have been prioritized above the line get done, and things below the line get done later. These are the problems you will solve another day.

Prioritization can get tricky, and sometimes political. This is especially true when the review and approval process involves multiple businesses, decision-makers and executives. People have opinions. Sometimes you agree with them and sometimes you don't. And sometimes you don't get to vote. The key to effectively navigate these waters is to be clear in your approach:

- These are the objectives.
- This is how these strategies support the objective.
- This is how much money we have to spend.
- This is the return on investment for each strategy.

Having laid out an articulate, well thought out assessment of the options, you have done everything in your power to help the organization pick the problem they want to solve. Rest assured - there will always be more problems to solve. Can you think back to a situation where prioritization would have helped you more effectively achieve your objective? I know I can.

6 Get to Know Your Customers

There is an important distinction between describing your customers and "getting to know" your customers

It is commonly understood among marketers that, in order to develop a message that will be heard by customers, you have to be able to describe who your customers are. Unfortunately, it isn't always common practice to do the work required to really understand your customers.

"Customer-centric." "Customer-driven." "Customer-focused." All of these phrases have been used to describe different approaches to understanding customers. There is an important distinction between describing your customers and "getting to know" your customers.

Most companies can describe their customers at some level. Usually these descriptions go something like this: "Our target customers are male college-students, age 18-24, with annual income of less than $15,000 per year."

This type of demographic data[2] (age, sex, location, decision-makers, influencers, vertical markets, company-size, or revenue) is descriptive of a type of customer, or group of customers. It certainly helps you understand who they are. But it doesn't help you "get to know" them.

Psychographic data[3], on the other hand, helps us understand the "why" behind the demographics. Psychographics focuses on attributes like personality, values, attitudes, interests, or lifestyles.

Psychographic profiles are really helpful when you are trying to define more personalized and targeted messages and campaigns. Continuing with our college student example, a psychographic description might be, "Male college students who are socially active and have a specific interest in the outdoors and extreme sports."

Finally, there are behavioral attributes[4]. As the name implies, these attributes refer to a person's behavior - or their actions or reactions to different products, messages, offers, etc. Behaviors can be either conscious or subconscious and provide an important final piece of information needed to "get to know" your customers. Back to our college student, "male college students in this target are extremely brand loyal and are usually familiar with this type of product."

Demographics = Who
Psychographics = Why
Behaviors = What

So a profile of the customer goes like this: Our target customers are male college-students, age 18-24, with annual income of less than $15,000 per year. These students are socially active and have a specific interest in the outdoors and extreme sports. They are extremely brand loyal and are familiar with this type of product."

This description has details that will help you focus on the way you reach this target. Plus, it sheds some light into the messages they might respond to.

You know how important it is to understand your customers. Armed with this kind of information you can go out there and "get to know" them a bit better.

NOTE Check out the Customer Profile Template at www.lauralowell.com/products.

7 Target Your Messages

You can sell more efficiently because you are targeting the right customer with the right product, with the right message in the right way

You know the old saying in the real estate business - "The three most important things in real estate are location, location, location." In marketing the three most important things are targeting, targeting and targeting.

To create targeted messages, you first have to identify your audience - who are you talking to? You can use a variety of data (demographic, psychographic and behavioral - refer to Rule 6) to divide your customers into distinct groups based on similar characteristics, needs or actions. By design, each group has fairly similar needs, so you can assume they will respond consistently to a given marketing tactic. They are likely to have common reactions, feelings and ideas about a specific message. They are likely to respond in a fairly predictable way to a marketing campaign focused on a specific product, sold at a given price, and distributed and promoted in a certain way.

In order for this approach to really work, you need to understand some things about each of your targets:

- What are the similarities within the group? How are individuals within the group alike? What is common among them?
- What are the differences between the groups? How do the groups distinguish themselves?

- How large is each group? Can you reasonably estimate the size of the group? Can this be validated?
- How accessible is each group? Is there a direct (or indirect) way to reach the group?

Use this kind of targeting to improve the focus and impact of your marketing activities. Understanding how different groups of customers perceive their problems helps you define your messages more clearly. Understanding behavior helps you to select the right marketing activities to reach your customers.

For example, let's say you are selling a hardware product to mid-sized companies. Within each of these companies are several people you need to get messages to in order to make a sale. There is the CIO who cares about the business impact of the solution; there is the VP of IT who cares about the operational and technical issues; and there is the IT Manager who is really focused on implementation and ongoing maintenance. Your message to the company should be consistent - we can help you solve your problem (for example). The individual communications to each target audience should be tailored to its unique needs, perceptions and business challenges. You don't want to talk to the CIO about maintenance schedules and upgrade plans, and the IT Manager probably doesn't care about financing options.

Technology also allows you to target your messages in ways we couldn't even dream of before we had the Internet. One of the challenges marketers have is how to manage your customer lists. How do you segment your lists in a meaningful way without ending up with multiple competing, overlapping and sometimes redundant lists?

With marketing automation tools today, you can directly "tag" your customers to indicate what they've done, what they've recently bought, what they did on your website, and so on. With this information you can specifically target your communications to them. You can communicate to your customers in ways that matter to them. And your messages are more effective at breaking through because your customers are actually interested in what you have to say.

Targeting can significantly increase your ability to close the deal. It can help you increase revenue and profitability. You can sell more efficiently because you are targeting the right customer with the right product, with the right message in the right way. After all, isn't that the point?

8 Customers Are People Too

A Persona is a detailed account of the daily life of a fictional customer

Statistics and data are useful in helping us paint a picture of who your customers are, what they value and how you can expect them to behave. But at some level it is very impersonal. You talk about your customers in very generic terms. You don't connect with them as individuals.

The only way to be heard is to make this data more personal. "Persona-based marketing" goes beyond simple data. It describes the qualities and characteristics of an average person who would fit the segment profile. It's like creating a character to play a role described by the profile.

Persona-based marketing describes who a prospect or customer is, by answering questions such as: What keeps this person awake at night? How do they spend their time? How do they like to receive information?

Personas create a dramatic, concrete portrait of your customers. It allows you to build a marketing message that's relevant to them and their lives. A Persona is a detailed account of the daily life of a fictional customer. It is usually written in real-life terms, even going so far as to give a personal name to each Persona. Persona descriptions typically include:

- A day in the life scenario
- Daily work activities

- Household and leisure activities
- Goals, fears, and aspirations
- Computer skills, knowledge, and abilities
- Market influence
- Demographic attributes (age, marital status, religion, etc.)
- Psychographics attributes (lifestyle, values, beliefs)
- Technology attitudes
- Communication methods
- Cultural considerations
- Personal quotes

Back in the mid-1990s, I worked in a start-up division of HP, called the Network Server Division (NSD). The business was growing like crazy. They had created the category (industry-standard servers), were leaders in the industry and had a "first-mover" advantage. What they didn't have was a creative marketing platform.

The marketing team created three very distinct Personas: Small- Office Sal, Server Sam and MIS Michelle. These three personalities represented their three target customer segments of small office, mid-range and enterprise businesses.

Sal, Sam and Michelle were our friends. We understood them, we knew what their issues were, and we knew what kept them up at night. In fact, the three of them were turned into life-size cardboard cut-outs that would join the team for division coffee talks, make appearances at executive review meetings and hang around the cubes in engineering, marketing and R&D.

These personas had such an impact on the employees that almost 10 years later when one of the veteran NSD employees was retiring, a search was conducted to find the posters of Sal, Sam and Michelle for the retirement party. Granted, Sal, Sam and Michelle were not real people. But they were invited nonetheless.

Referring to them as colleagues and friends helped the team to develop and execute messages that made the marketing more effective. It helped move the entire business away from conversations about what we thought internally, towards conversations that focused on what our customers would think. Whenever the team was faced with a challenging decision, someone would always ask "What would Sal think?" or "How would Michelle react to this?" The personas we created kept us focused and pointed in the right direction.

9 See the Forest and the Trees

It's important to look beyond the walls of your cubicle and get a sense of what is going on around you

Your customers have many options. It is up to you to communicate to them in context of the overall universe of possibilities - the market in which you operate. Your job is to convince customers that your product, service or solution is obviously the best choice for them.

Understanding how your company, product or service stacks up against the competition is a logical step towards creating a message that is convincing and compelling.

Marketing strategy guru Jack Trout said "differentiate or die." That doesn't mean bashing the competition. It does mean knowing your relative strengths and weaknesses and positioning your offer accordingly. It's important to look beyond the walls of your cubicle and get a sense of what is going on around you. It is sometimes really easy to get caught up in the internal perceptions of the market.

For example, you have probably heard people say something like "that new standard will never get adopted - they don't have enough support from partners." Maybe so, but it is a good idea to stick your head out the window every once in a while and see if what you believe is really true. Otherwise, you might find yourself at a distinct disadvantage.

Look for external market influences and how they might affect your company and the competition. Consider the political, economic, social and technical issues surrounding your customers including regulatory requirements and even international trade issues. How about political affiliations? Are economic factors like inflation or interest rates a major concern to your customers?

What are the technological trends in the industry? Can you claim leadership? Do your customers value that leadership? How can you position developments in the category in the best light possible for your customers? How can you make things better for them than any of their other alternatives?

MetaLINCS is a provider of electronic discovery software. They launched their product in 2006 into an established, multi-billion dollar but risk-averse legal and investigatory services industry. MetaLINCS felt their new technology would revolutionize the e-discovery market. To their surprise, their target customers weren't ready to be revolutionized.

The traditional e-discovery business model was built on manual review of electronic documents by relatively low-paid young associates or paralegals. Automating this process cuts directly into law firm and services companies' revenues, and enterprises weren't yet compelled to perform this function in-house. After launching to an intrigued but slow-to-act market, the company found that their highest impact would come from institutional influencers like the Department of Justice. They re-vamped their go-to-market strategy and went after the DOJ and the supplier vendors to convince them to use the MetaLINCS product as the e-discovery platform of choice. Now they are one of the approved reporting standards for e discovery in DOJ investigations. They have increased their penetration rates and their sales funnel and revenue stream is steadily growing.

What started out as a flop - has been turned into a huge success. These are the moments when it is more important than ever to take a look around and see the forest and the trees.

10 Change the Words, Not the Idea

There is a difference between messages and copy. A message is an idea or concept that you communicate to a target audience through a variety of activities. Copy is the articulation of the message for a specific activity.

Message = Idea
Copy = Words

For example, a message or idea may be "Ease of Use." Look at the tremendously memorable copy created by Geico Insurance: "It's so easy, even a caveman could do it." The message is ease of use, but the copy is very creative, clever and easy to remember. The copy conveys the idea and may or may not use the specific words. The same message is communicated in their "Gecko" ads as well. Same idea, different copy (and creative, by the way).

Copy can and should change frequently. Messages should not. Copy should reflect current industry trends, cultural icons and social phenomena. Messages should focus on a single core idea. This may sound like a contradiction, but in fact it is an important distinction. The core idea your company or product stands for is fundamental to your business strategy. Therefore, shifting this message should be considered in the same league as shifting your business strategy.

Unfortunately, sometimes you get bored with your messages. You spend hours fine-tuning and testing them. Finally, by the time your campaigns launch and the message is out there, it feels old and stale to you. But you have to remember that your customers are just beginning to see the messages and that it takes a while for them to get through. Even though you're bored, your customers are not. They need to see your messages over and over again for them to register. Not necessarily the same words, but the same idea supported by the same brand.

You wouldn't change business strategies just because you're bored, yet marketers change their messages all the time to their detriment. You want to keep the message fresh and alive by changing the copy. This means using unusual language, a clever play on words, or a connection to a current event in your copy that adds life to a message while giving it some "staying power."

Again, the Geico example is a case where the message is very common and could be applied to many different companies. However, clever use of language makes the copy unique and helps Geico stand out in a crowd. The "caveman" and "Gecko" characters add a very unique and personal element to the message.

Make your copy memorable, interesting, and quotable. People can remember "It's so easy a caveman can do it." It becomes a commonly-used phrase that people begin to use in everyday life. How cool is that?

NOTE Check out the Messaging Template at www.lauralowell.com/products.

11 Involve Them and They Will Understand

Involve your customers in a dialogue. Show them your products, your facilities and your people

Confucius said "Tell me and I'll forget. Show me and I'll remember. Involve me and I'll understand." He was a smart guy.

There are basically three ways your potential customers learn about your business:

- They hear one of your messages directly.
- They are told about an experience someone else had.
- They have an experience with your company.

It is generally understood that if someone has a negative experience with your product, brand or company, they are far more likely to tell someone about it. That means it is even more important to help customers have positive experiences. These experiences can range from buying the product in a store, online, of from a global account rep - was it a good experience? What about once you get the product? What was it like to open the box (I hate those clam shells that require garden shears to open)? These things might seem insignificant, but in the customers mind they make a huge difference. These are the things they remember and will tell their friends and colleagues about. Good or bad is up to you.

Your message and the experiences you create are the common threads that tie these three things together. Think about it. As a consumer of stuff don't you appreciate it when you get to experience something first hand before buying it? Why wouldn't your customers - business and consumer - appreciate the same thing?

Flexperience Staffing, a start-up company in the Silicon Valley, specializes in flexible staffing services for marketing, human resource and finance functions for clients that need part-time, flex-time or project-based resources. CEO and co-founder, Sally Thornton, created an experience for her clients - the New Formula for Success conference. The conference brought together women who are successfully working in part-time or flexible work assignments with women who wanted to be. The panelists had "been there and done that" and were able to share what they learned to make flexible work schedules work for them.

Sally and her team had expected about 150 people to attend. The week before the event registrations were at 400. The day of the event they had almost 450 attendees. The experience of getting together with other people with similar interests and needs was extremely compelling.

But you don't have to get people into a room to share an experience. Technology enables you to offer online, real-time demos of your products. You can give virtual tours to customers in Maine, US of your manufacturing facilities located in Penang, Malaysia. You can download a free trial version of the latest multi-player car racing game. The possibilities are amazing.

Involve your customers in a dialogue. Show them your products, your facilities and your people. Pull them in to something that matters to them and they will understand (and remember).

12 Be Different

Differentiation is the way you go about separating your product from the crowd so it is more attractive to your potential customers

Differentiators are, by definition, those things that make your company, product or service different. Today in high-tech industries, technology at a product level is usually only a short-term differentiator. In consumer markets things like product design or brand image can be very compelling differentiators. Just consider the Apple iPhone.

As a phone, it is much like other phones on the market — you can check email, view your calendar, and take pictures. There are definitely some technological advances, but it is the design and image of the iPhone that make it such a coveted status symbol.

Differentiation is the way you go about separating your product from the crowd so it is more attractive to your potential customers. Not only do you need to differentiate your product from the competition, but also from your other products that might serve a similar need. The objective is to create a position for your product (or company) that others perceive as unique.

There are a lot of ways to differentiate your company or products. Branding has been used by many established brands to differentiate among their own products. Toothpaste is a great example. How many version of Crest or Colgate can there possibly be? Yet there is differentiation in packaging, merchandising and branding between Crest with Tartar Control and Crest Whitening. These products serve different markets with different needs.

Another popular approach to differentiation is technology. Unfortunately, as soon as you do something great with technology, someone is going to come along and copy what you've done and make it better, faster and/or cheaper[5]. Then you have lost your differentiator. You have to start over again, and it becomes a game of leapfrog.

Quality can be a powerful differentiator but only in markets where quality is a really powerful customer desire. Medical equipment, for example, is heavily reliant on both product quality and brand image. In the toothpaste example, quality ingredients are important factors to some consumers. They might prefer Tom's of Maine toothpaste whose differentiator is natural, quality ingredients.

Promotional activities and incentives can also serve to differentiate products. These tactics tend to have a very short-term impact on sales figures - purchases pick up when there is a promotion or special. Then as soon as the promotion is over, purchase rates go back to their former levels. Not a bad thing, but you need to understand the dynamics of promotions in order to use them as a differentiator.

Where do you start? What do you do to actually differentiate your products? Well, you can start by summarizing what you know about your customer's problems, challenges, needs and fears. Follow that with a short description of how your product addresses what your customer needs and how it makes their life better. Map this against your customers' alternatives - the competition. This is where you find your real differentiators. They are often not technological, but rather business differentiators like service, quality, efficiency, relationships, and so on.

If nothing jumps out at you, then you have an interesting piece of information. Look beyond the basics. Look for opportunities "outside the box" and you might be surprised by what you find.

13 Admit When You Make a Mistake

Most customers would rather know the truth and work with you to find a solution

Mistakes happen. It's one thing to forget to update the slide presentation to include a late-breaking piece of data. But what if you ship wine that goes bad in transit? What if you mess up and end up on the evening news because you left millions of customers stranded? Not fun, but it does happen.

In 1979, after spending six years building Navarro Vineyards, Ted Bennett was ready to begin broadly distributing his wines. He focused primarily on Pinot Noir and Gewürztraminer, varietals not common in the late 1970s.

Ted and his wife Deborah needed a way to get people to taste these new wines. They came up with a plan. First, they decided to open a Tasting Room at the vineyard. The Tasting Room opened in 1980 and began to draw quite a following. By 1982, they started their pre-release offering, and by 1984 they had a loyal customer base.

Second, they began to target local restaurants using their network in the San Francisco Bay Area. Their first restaurant customer was Alice Waters, owner of Chez Panisse in Berkeley, California. Once they were on the wine list at Chez

Panisse, they started to get calls from other well-known restaurants and their brand of boutique wines began to gain broader appeal.

Several years later, Navarro had produced a long-awaited unfiltered Gewürztraminer. After it was bottled, the team found that there were some residual sugars in the wine that fermented after it was shipped (as part of the pre-release). Oh no...the wine had "gone off."

Ted and company contacted all of their pre-release customers directly, and offered a credit on the wine. Few (if any) of the customers accepted the credit. They did appreciate the call and the honesty. Be open and honest and treat your customers with respect. They usually are willing to forgive an honest mistake.

Jet Blue, a well known low-cost US airline, experienced a major meltdown of its infrastructure during an ice storm in February 2007. After the massive ice storm hit the east coast of the United States, almost 1,000 flights ended up being cancelled over a six-day period. Passengers were trapped on runways for hours without food, water or working toilets. How would you like to be the one trying to explain this to your customers (not to mention the press)?

Well, David Neeleman was the guy with that honor. He is the CEO of Jet Blue and the one in the hot seat. He had a decision to make; admit Jet Blue made a mistake and make it right, or, start making excuses and try to blame it on the weather.

It's a good thing for Jet Blue that David is a pretty smart guy. It took him a few days to figure out what was going on, but not only did he publicly apologize, on The Late Show with David Letterman no less, but he sent a direct email message to customers that said "We are sorry and embarrassed. But most of all, we are deeply sorry." It is hard not to accept such an apology.

These are definitely extreme examples. But most customers would rather know the truth and work with you to find a solution. A long list of excuses and finger-pointing isn't going to get you very far in the long-run. Although it is sometimes easier than actually saying "We're sorry."

14 Messages Need Testing Too

Keep in mind, just because people inside the company think the messages are "on target" doesn't mean your customers do

Some companies are hesitant to approach customers for "message testing." If you work with your customers to understand what they need and then deliver it, why would those same customers not want to help explain what you do to other customers? Call me crazy, but I've rarely had customers say "No" when they've been asked to contribute their ideas to a messaging study.

The idea of testing can be scary - what if you don't pass? What if you decide to go with a message that you and your team like, but your customers don't understand? Which is worse?

Testing should be done in stages. Begin with an informal discussion with valued customers. You want to understand what they think about your company, your products, your service, your employees, and your executives. You don't get this type of insight through an online survey or focus group. Early in the process is the time to gather possible messaging ideas straight from your customers.

The most effective approach is to use customer interviews to gather the feedback you need. Typically, interviews of this nature are 30-60 minutes, either face-to-face or on the phone (the latter is becoming much more common). Here are a few potential open-ended interview questions for early-stage message testing:

* What do you think is the main idea behind each message?
* What do these messages mean to you?
* Are these messages important to you?
* How do these messages satisfy your needs?
* Why are these messages believable and credible?
* How do these messages differentiate our offering?

The outcome of these interviews will cause you to look at your messages differently. At this point, you want to take the input that is most relevant, integrate the feedback into your message options and start the more formal process of actually testing possible messages.

When people think of "market research" they often think of expensive, complicated approaches involving focus groups, interviews or other high-touch methods. The truth is you don't have to invest millions in market research to validate that you're on the right track.

A combination of qualitative and quantitative analysis is best, but it's not always possible. Qualitative research includes focus groups, one-on-one interviews and such. Quantitative research usually involves surveys where the responses are mostly closed-ended (meaning they have fixed responses to choose from).

The most important aspect of message testing is to test with a significant enough sample of your target audience. A sample of 300 will result in a "statistically significant" result; however a sample of 30 will result in solid understanding of the target to within one standard deviation. Do you remember the lectures about "N" in your statistics class in college? If you have a nice big budget, then you can afford N=300. Otherwise, N=30 is just fine for directional guidance. For most start-ups and smaller companies the difference between 30 and 300 does not warrant the extra investment.

Regardless of how you do the testing, the results you find can either validate your messages, or give you new insights and direction to keep you from making avoidable mistakes. Keep in mind, just because people inside the company think the messages are "on target" doesn't mean your customers do.

NOTE Check out the Message Testing Template at www.lauralowell.com/products.

15 Just Say No to Jargon

The point is, make sure what you write actually means something

This rule will empower you to leverage your thinking and step outside the box so that you can help customers find solutions to their problems. Huh?

In an effort to sound smart, different and credible, the language of corporate marketing has taken a turn for the worse. Complete websites, brochures and datasheets are written that don't mean a darn thing. We understand all the words, but when they are put together we don't know what it means. What, for example does "we provide technical solutions for progressive companies" mean? How about; "technical innovation is the foundation of our best-in-class industry leading solutions that exceeds customers' expectations." What in the world does this actually mean?

This type of corporate gobbledygook is not helpful. In fact, it has just the opposite affect. Customers read your brochure (or website or white paper) and are left with more questions than answers. Since it would require effort on their part to figure out what you do, they move on to the next guy - and you've lost a potential customer.

It isn't very often that a customer says to themselves, "I need an innovative solution to exceed my expectations." They probably think "I've been trying really hard to solve this problem and I just can't - maybe someone else can help."

So what is a marketer to do? Well, some clever folks at Deloitte Consulting took it upon themselves to create "BullFighter"[6] - a clever piece of software that looks at all your copy and identifies all the "bull words."

The software plugs in to Microsoft Word and works much like spell-check or grammar-check. You select "Bullfighter" and it finds "bull words" and suggests alternatives. Just for fun, I did a before and after test of several phrases. This is what I got:

Stakeholder: Alternative words were vampire slayer, victim and forks. "Overused to the point of pain by consultants."

First-Mover: "Battle cry from the first Internet boom-bust, one with little remaining credibility."

Empower: "A grandiose word...solidly enshrined in the Consulting Cliché Hall of Fame."

Hatsize Learning Corporation took this lesson to heart when they revised their corporate positioning and messages. Initially their top three messages were: optimize resources & hardware; reduce delivery costs; and increase training revenue. After much discussion the team found the underlying benefits and got straight to the point. Their new message is: more revenue, higher margins through increased product knowledge. The impact was to get away from buzz-words that mean nothing and say what you really want to say.

The point is, make sure what you write actually means something. Make sure it means something to someone who doesn't work for your company. Make sure it means something to your customers and potential customers. How do you know? Just ask them.

16 Be Compelling

All your customers think about is how your company (or product) can help them

You heard it before: "This copy just isn't compelling" or "We need something more compelling." That's all well and good, but how in the world do you create a compelling message and copy?

First, write all of your marketing pieces like you're talking to your customers. Don't talk from the company's point of view. Customers don't care about why the company thinks this is a good idea, or why the company decided to pursue this strategy. All your customers think about is how your company (or product) can help them.

As you go through the process of developing your messages remember to ask yourself the age-old question "What's in it for me?" "Me" in this case is your customer.

- How does it benefit me?
- How does it solve my problem?
- How is it different from my other options?

> WIIFM =
> "What's in it for me?"

Second, talk about something your customers actually care about, not what you think they care about. Based on "what's in it for them" you can talk about how your product will help them. Stay away from features - this is really hard for product marketing people. Your product is like your child, and you know how hard it is not to talk about your kids. But you have to try. Take your incredible features and talk about how they directly help customers. Your feature might be "fastest product on the market." The benefit to the customer is that it saves them time.

Third, try and make it personal. Ask customers a question to help them identify the challenges they might be facing. Sometimes customers don't know they have a problem until you ask the question. Then they think "Interesting - I hadn't thought of it that way - I should investigate that idea." Now you've started the ball rolling and can go back to the customers and nurture the idea along.

It is also helpful to use other customers to validate your message. Messages are always more compelling when they come from someone like them - your customers. If I tell you I'm cool, I therefore am definitely anything but cool. But if someone else like you tells you I'm cool, then I probably am. Stories, quotes, anecdotes, success stories, case studies - call them whatever you like - they are all very effective at telling your customers you're cool without your having to say you're cool.

Finally, always have a call to action (see Rule 25.) Different customers are going to connect with different benefits of your message (or product). This means that you should have several prompts in each marketing piece. Every time you highlight a benefit, follow it up with a prompt to "buy now" or "learn more" or "contact us" or "try a free demo" - you get the point. You might actually have several prompts in a single marketing piece. Don't let that bother you. If your customer doesn't know what to do next, then you've lost them. Walk them through the process and give them something to do each step if the way.

This approach might feel too direct. It might be perceived as too obvious in some industries. But think of it this way - if a customer doesn't know what's in it for them, and they don't know what to do about it, all your work up to that point is for nothing.

Do It Their Way

No one likes to be asked for their preferences or opinions and then have them ignored

Before you can create a marketing mix that really works, you need to know two very important things. First, how do your customers gather information? Who do they go to for recommendations? Do they search online or do they ask for suggestions from colleagues, friends or family? Who influences the purchasing process? Answers to these questions help you target those who influence your customers, as well as the customers themselves.

Second, how do your target customers want to receive information? Do they want a lot of detail but not very often? Do they prefer to get more frequent information with less detail? Do they like phone, email or old-fashioned paper and envelopes? Again, this information will directly impact the types of marketing activities you invest in.

Once these preferences have been stated, it is your job to execute them consistently. No one likes to be asked for their preferences or opinions and then have them ignored.

eBay has taken this approach when they talk to different groups of eBay users. Within eBay, there are the obvious groupings of "buyers" and "sellers." Then there are the different types of buyers ranging from casual to hard core; and the different types of sellers, including folks like me who have sold something once or twice for fun and other sellers eBay refers to as "power-sellers." Some of these folks can sell over a million dollars of merchandise a month on the site.

Constructing the optimal mix is part art (see Rule 34) and part science (see Rule 35.) The art lies in understanding the nuances between the different marketing activities, how to craft copy tailored to the marketing activity, and how to combine copy with creative for optimal impact. The science lies in the measurement and tracking of the effectiveness of various activities at delivering your message to your target audience.

The important thing to remember is to put yourself in your customer's place. Think of an outstanding experience you have had with a company- the company seemed to know a lot about you, they followed-up in an appropriate way, they were able to anticipate what you needed every step of the way.

Now, think of the opposite experience where it seemed like the company didn't have a clue who they were talking to. Their messages were irrelevant, out of context or just plain stupid. This experience also stands out, but for the wrong reasons.

Your goal is to create a marketing mix that reaches your customers in ways that are appropriate for them. Find out who influences your customers and make them love you. Find out how your customers like to hear from you and be zealous in your attempt to abide by their wishes. They will thank you for it with increased sales and impressive loyalty.

18 Be Consistent

Your messages need to be integrated into every customer interaction

The American Heritage Dictionary defines consistency as follows: con·sis·ten·cy: Agreement or logical coherence among things or parts. If you want your marketing to work double-time for you, you need to consistently communicate your message so that customers have the chance to hear you, internalize the message and then act on it.

Your messages need to be integrated into every customer interaction. You don't need to use the same words over and over. However, each communication needs to reinforce the core idea that has been developed to support your strategy. It is a case where the whole is greater than the sum of the parts - when the messages are consistently conveyed across multiple interactions, and the customer is left with a clear understanding of what the company, product, service, or solution is, and how it solves their problem.

Let's say there's a great article in a trade publication that mentions your company and your new product. A customer reads it. Then at an industry tradeshow your company has a booth and is hosting a panel discussion. The customer attends. They also see the small ad you placed in an industry trade publication coinciding with the tradeshow. "Interesting," they think to themselves as they enter your company name into the Google search box. Their search produces a link to your latest white paper, which they download.

The next day, the customer receives an email from your company thanking them for their interest and for downloading the white paper. The email includes a link to a customized landing page with their name thanking them for attending the tradeshow and downloading the white paper. You have a great offer for them on your newest product...and the story continues. With consistent use of key messages across multiple touch-points, your customers come away with the sense that your company is worth their consideration.

The opposite scenario is played out over and over again by companies trying to "punch up" their copy or "update" their collateral. It is usually done with the best of intentions, but when you start making "minor little adjustments" there are often unintended consequences.

For example, you update your datasheet to contain the latest product image. In the process you come up with a clever new phrase to describe the product, so you go ahead and add it to the datasheet to keep things fresh. Unfortunately, the datasheet is part of your customer welcome kit that uses the original product description as part of the headline.

Not only is the datasheet disconnected from the other materials the customer receives, it is confusing. Not only did you lose a chance to reinforce one key idea, but you raised more questions than you answered.

From the company tagline to your email signature; from the CEO's keynote to your e-newsletter, press releases, website and advertising, your message must be communicated consistently in order to be heard.

Use the Right Tools

Images, music, and voices – they change the way you think about the story you're telling, and how you tell it

You constantly hear about the latest new marketing trends and the coolest new technologies. As cool as they are, these things are only useful if your target customers use them.

It is critical to the success of your marketing campaign that you identify customer-preferred vehicles and prioritize them above "really hot" things. While these may be the latest trend, they may not produce the results you want.

There is no easy recipe for how to create the perfect mix. Much like the perfect chocolate chip cookie — it can be different for everyone. Marketing vehicles are the butter, flour, sugar and eggs that make up our marketing mix. Depending on how we combine them we can get soft, chewy or crispy cookies. Depending on how we combine different marketing vehicles we can address awareness, demand generation or lead conversion objectives. Even though the ingredients are the same, the results are different.

The other thing to think about is the way your activities are communicated. The world has moved way beyond traditional text-based communications. Now you need to think about how to use a variety of media, including video and audio, to best communicate your message. Mary Beth

Garber, President of the Southern California Broadcasters Association observed that there are definitely parallels to the traditional marketing: audio is like radio; video is like TV; and text is like print.

> Audio = Radio
> Video = TV
> Text = Print

However, with the explosive growth of online video sharing sites like YouTube these distinctions quickly become blurred. You can embed audio help files on your website. You can create a video "Getting Started Guide" for your customers. The possibilities are endless.

The challenge lies in how to translate what we currently do into these new formats. Ms. Garber also noted that "Radio is the only medium that transfers directly to the internet without changing format. Radio...listeners don't differentiate between FM, AM, XM or streaming online." It is an interesting and useful observation. What was once seen as a declining medium is in fact on the forefront. The use of audio online is increasingly becoming the norm with many marketers. Plus, the distinction between online and offline mediums are quickly becoming blurred.

You can and should be using these different mediums to communicate in creative ways that differentiate you from the competition. However, that doesn't mean that everyone needs to go out right now and create a corporate video or podcast.

What it does mean is that you need to begin thinking very differently about what you do. You can move beyond words to tell your story. Images, music, and voices - they change the way you think about the story you're telling, and how you tell it.

NOTE Check out the Marketing Mix Template at www.lauralowell.com/products.

Rule 19: Use the Right Tools

20 See and Be Seen

Visibility means you can be found when someone is looking for you

Whether you're a new business (start-up, consultant or mom & pop shop), an existing business just beginning to develop an online presence, or a large business that's been around forever, what you care about is being visible.

Visibility means you can be found when someone is looking for you; that you are where they are; and that you appear when they are looking for things related to what you do. Visibility is a function of placement and messages.

In order for your business to be heard, you have to be in the right places. That means you need to be where your customers are looking (placement). Where do customers go for information? Who are the credible influencers in your industry? Are there key magazines, trade associations or forums where your customers gather? This is where you want to be. Identifying these places is the first step towards helping customers know you exist.

These places are both real and virtual, offline and online. Many companies think they can have a purely online marketing strategy. After all, it is much more cost-effective. On the other hand, not everyone hangs out on the Internet waiting to be bombarded with messages about your product. Some people still go to conferences, tradeshows and real life face-to-face meetings.

When you find their hang-outs (either real or virtual), do what it takes to be really visible in those places. Having a booth at a tradeshow is one thing. Having a booth, facilitating a workshop, placing an ad in the daily and a hosting a customer luncheon tells a much different, and more compelling, story. You're everywhere and people will know you exist.

Once your customers find you, you need to have content they find valuable and compelling (messages). You want your message to be relevant.

What you say has to address something that is important to your customers, like a piece of information they can actually use or a referral to a resource who might be a good reference for them. If you can provide helpful information, then you become valuable and they will remember what you had to say - "Oh yeah, that's the guy who gave me the great article on enterprise compliance - that was really helpful."

Then it becomes a matter of asking your customers to take the next step. That next step can be clicking a link to learn more, downloading a white paper or article, returning a registration card, or calling you directly.

It isn't easy. Half the battle of executing effective marketing campaigns is being in the right place. The other half is having a message customers remember once they find you.

21 Blogs are Good

Blogs are a great way to promote your ideas and opinions and get others to join your conversation

Blogs are a great way to promote your ideas and opinions and get others to join your conversation. Blogs are similar to message-boards in that they usually focus on a specific topic, but blogs are much more friendly and personal. They are your platform to speak your mind, share ideas and elicit comments from others.

Blogs are also a great way to get your content picked up by the search engines. Technically, blogs are very effective for distributing searchable user-generated content. This is important for search engine marketing (SEM) because the more content you have the better your search results will be. If you have a blog on your website, you have more opportunities to add content that the search engines consider valuable.

Before you start your blog, be clear about why you are doing it. What are you trying to accomplish? Blogs are great at increasing awareness of you, your company or your product. They aren't so great at generating demand or converting leads into sales.

Once you're clear about why you're going to start a blog, consider who your readers will be, and what types of things might interest them.

Personal blogs tend to have a "diary/journal" feel to them, and people tend to write whatever is on their mind, interesting things that happened that day. Although, truth be told, the play-by-play of what someone's cat did last Thursday doesn't work for everyone.

For a business blog, this isn't the most productive approach. Focusing on a specific topic or idea that is relevant to your business and meaningful to your customers is a better bet. Things like "marketing for small business" or "compliance requirements in the energy industry" or "compensation strategies" would be more appropriate for a business blog. But that doesn't mean it has to be boring and overly-corporate.

On the other hand, blogs are by their nature very personal. As a result, it is pretty common for bloggers to go off on a tangent every now and again. Frankly, this is when some of the most interesting discussions take place. These digressions make the blog more interesting. You see the "real" side of a business issue and give the reader insight into what it is really like to be the CIO or software engineer or graphic designer.

Now that you know why you're writing a blog, who you're writing it for and what your topic is, you need to select a blogging tool. There are a number of resources for creating a blog, and the most popular ones are pretty similar. A very comprehensive comparison has been developed by The Annenberg Center for Communication at USC:
http://www.ojr.org/ojr/images/blog_software_comparison.cfm

The platform you select will be a function of what features you prefer, how easy the tool is to use, and of course, the cost of the platform. Most services have both a free and paid version of their tools. The free versions are great when you're just starting out, but they tend to be more limited in their layout and color options. This can be a problem if you're integrating to an existing website. If not, then you may not care.

Now that the technical issues are taken care of, it is time to start writing. The moment you've been waiting for, or maybe not. First-time bloggers are often intimidated by the blank screen and the fear of putting their ideas out there. If this is how you feel, try writing a little "hello, welcome to my blog" paragraph and post it to your blog. Then you can add a little more about yourself, your background, your company...and with a little practice, the ideas will start flowing. After all, you're a marketer.

22 Email is Personal

With behavioral marketing, the customer dictates the messages they receive from you based on what they are doing

A single email can sometimes be the difference between winning and losing a sale. Then why are up to 89 percent of marketers still using canned broadcast emails?[7]

Behavioral targeting has been used by advertisers for years. The idea is to observe a customers behavior and then provide the appropriate ad based on what they did or didn't do. This concept can, and should, be applied to email marketing in a much more comprehensive way.

The idea is to track a customer's behavior and modify your marketing to reflect what is relevant to them based on their behavior or actions. This approach allows you to serve up marketing messages, offers and promotions that are more relevant and compelling to the specific customer. Cool, huh?

There are even software tools available to track customer patterns (online and offline) so that marketers can deliver personalized messages based on a sequence of actions taken by a unique customer. One company, MoonRay, has managed to integrate online and offline marketing better then most. Through a series of "tags" and codes, marketers are able to create a sequence of events based on the actions of a customer or potential customer. Everything from phone calls, emails and direct mail can be coordinated through the automated system.

What you find out about your customers can have a profound impact on how you market to them. In fact, this approach is almost the opposite of how most companies do email marketing today. With behavioral marketing, the customer dictates the messages they receive from you based on what they are doing. For example, if a customer visits your website several, but doesn't take you up on your offer, then you deliver a message that makes a suggestion. It is similar to the Amazon.com "People who bought this, also bought that" approach.

This is pretty powerful stuff especially when you consider that the success of an email marketing campaign is usually measured in terms of open rates and click-through rates. Open rates measure the number of times the email was opened. Click-through rates measure the number of times someone actually clicked on a link in the email.

If you make your messages more relevant, you increase your response rates. If you increase your response rate, you generate more qualified leads. If you generate more qualified leads, you close more deals and sell more products.

It doesn't matter whether your product is a $500,000 service contract on a customized software solution, or a $50 video game download. If you base your messages on your customer behavior the messages are more meaningful, and you will be more successful.

NOTE Register at www.42Rules.com and see MoonRay at work.

23 Viral Marketing is a Tactic

The things that typically take off are either tragically sad or hilariously funny

In terms of demand generation - viral marketing is a fascinating topic. There was an article in the Wall Street Journal that talked about the changing face of marketing, and how the Internet and viral elements have changed the nature of marketing forever. The Journal is right.

Viral marketing is related to search engine marketing, blogs and email marketing. It is really just an online version of good old-fashioned "word of mouth." The major difference, of course, is that it now takes seconds for an idea to spread versus days, weeks or months using the traditional "she tells two friends, and so on, and so on" method made famous by Breck shampoo commercials.

The objective of viral marketing is to seed your idea or message with key influencers in an online community with the hope that they will have good things to say about your product, service, company, etc. And you hope that they will spread the good news for you, like a virus.

A few years ago we were using the Internet to push info to customers and were enabling customers to find information about our products/services by publishing our info on the Web - we thought this was a huge change. We didn't have a clue what was coming.

Today, customers are publishing their own information about our products or services. User-generated content, social networking and online communities have turned everything inside-out. You are no longer in control of the messages. You can start the ball rolling, but once it's out there and customers begin to talk about you, it becomes a matter of influence, not control.

Targeting influencers who will (hopefully) comment positively on your product or service is an age-old strategy. Blogs, email, chat rooms and online communities make it faster, and allow it to grow bigger due to the reach of the Internet. The reason viral marketing works is based on human emotion. The things that typically take off are either tragically sad or hilariously funny.

During the holiday selling season in 2006, a cute little site called "Go Elf Yourself"[8] appeared. You could "elf yourself" by uploading a photo (of yourself or an unsuspecting friend or colleague), recording a short message and showing off with a funny little elf dance.

The site was the brainchild of Office Depot and was created as part of a multi-phased viral campaign that ended in January 2007 with a full-page ad in the Wall Street Journal. Office Depot apologized for their little game causing such a significant drop in productivity and invited businesses everywhere to come to Office Depot and stock up on productivity items. As far as results go, in mid-December 2006 the site was averaging 200 unique visitors per second; people were creating 8 new elves per second. That's a lot of elves.

The elves certainly didn't change the world. But the idea behind it certainly could.

24 Be Critical

**It is important
to ask for
other
people's
opinions**

It's easy to review your own material. It is easy to ask a colleague on your team to review it. In general, getting people to review your stuff is pretty easy. What's hard is being specific about the kind of help you need.

When you ask for "feedback" you are opening the door for all kinds of input. Almost everyone will provide grammar and punctuation edits whether you ask them to or not, and most of the time this isn't terribly helpful. Of course, you don't want typos in your materials, but a good copyeditor takes care of that. (And in case there is any doubt, you need a copyeditor, a real live editor who does copyediting for a living.)

Unfortunately, it is hard to describe the other type of help you need when reviewing and improving marketing materials. There are several questions I always ask when I'm asking people to review my stuff:

- Does the piece make sense?
- Did it flow? Was there a logical sequence of ideas?
- What was the key idea you took away from the piece?
- What do you wish was included that wasn't?

These questions, and others like them, provide specific guidance for the type of insight you're asking for. Otherwise, you're asking for help but not giving people enough information to actually make them helpful.

Now that you have the feedback you're looking for, what do you do with it? Well, first you read it and ask clarifying questions. It is a nice way of subconsciously thanking people for giving you their time and attention. A quick question lets them know that you read it and thought about their input. They are much more likely to help you again in the future if they know you actually looked at their input. It also helps you think through their ideas and make sure you really understand what they were saying.

The next step is to figure out what input is relevant and what input is personal or organizational bias. This part can get a bit sticky, especially if there are organizational issues going on behind the scenes. In any case, you have to wade through it and decide what you're going to use.

Finally, after all the ideas are in front of you, it is time to start making changes. Give yourself some time to do this. If your project is particularly complicated or if there is a lot of conflicting input, it helps to "sleep on it." I also find it useful to approach one of your reviewers and ask their thoughts on all the input you received - sometimes talking it through can unlock new ideas and give you a fresh perspective.

It is important to ask for others people's opinions. Acknowledge their help, and then do what is right for you and your customers. Speaking about customers, what do you think they would say about it? Are you "eating your own dog food?" Or have you really told a story that is clear, relevant and important to your customers? Only they know for sure.

25 Always Have a Next Step

Each suggested action has the potential to keep customers interested and moving down the road toward purchasing something from you

What do you want your customers to do? The most obvious answer is to buy your stuff. There are quite a few steps from a customer first learning about your company and your product to their actually purchasing something from you. Each and every communication with a customer should suggest the next step in the process. It needs to be crystal clear what you want your customers to do after they have heard from you.

The next step can be as simple as "call me with questions at 555-1212." It can be a link in an email directing them to download a white paper or view your product overview video. It can be an offer encouraging them to "Buy Now!"

First you have to make it clear what the next step is - or what their alternatives are. HP, for example, includes "Call, click or visit" in all of their advertising. This makes it clear to customers that they can call HP for information or answers to their questions, they can visit their website and get more insight, or they can go down to their local retailer and have a live conversation with someone who knows about HP products. Pretty clear what their options are.

Then you need to make sure it is easy for the customer to complete the next step. Is the phone number printed on your landing page and your brochure? Did you include a link to a map of your location in the email? Did you provide download instructions for the white paper? As soon as a customer has to spend more than 10 seconds thinking about how to do something - you run the risk of losing them. Each step has the potential to lose a certain percentage of your customers. Each suggested action has the potential to keep them interested and moving down the road toward purchasing something from you.

You've got their attention. They have taken the action you recommended. Now what? Well, this is the time to make them an offer that is valuable to them. It can be a free consultation, a subscription to your latest research results, or an invitation to an executive roundtable breakfast meeting where they get the inside scoop on the industry. The options are limited only by your creativity. This is not the time to send out discounts, rebates or incentives. The customer is interested; they have taken a step forward.

The time to offer price incentives is when they have their foot in the door, yet they decide to leave. This is the perfect time to offer a discount on a bundle - "If you buy these two items, we'll give you a 25% discount on the total price." You can also offer instant rebates "Buy now and save 10%." You can also add incremental services or support - "This price also includes an extended warranty on all products and an upgrade to our service package."

At this point, you still need to include a specific action for the customer to take. This is not only limited to website, landing pages and direct marketing. The same principles can be used in sales presentations, telemarketing and relationship building. If you meet a potential customer for lunch to discuss the objectives of their project, what expectations do you set for next steps? You can offer to send the customer some background information (articles relevant to their project, or an interesting website that they might find useful). You can suggest a next meeting or a follow-up phone call.

Whatever you do, always make sure that your customers know the next step. If they don't know what to do next, they probably won't.

26 Change is Your Friend

Keeping up with the latest news and information isn't just a nice-to-have — It is a requirement for most marketers

For some people, staying up with the latest and greatest industry trends and happenings is second nature. For some it is a painful requirement of the job that never seems to get as much attention as it should.

You know that you should eat less and exercise more - but that doesn't mean you actually do it (at least not all the time). You know you should read the blogs and keep up on who was acquired or who closed up shop.

Keeping up with the latest news and information isn't just a nice-to-have. It is a requirement for most marketers. You need to know what is going on in your industry so that you can position and message your company appropriately when the dynamics change.

What would happen if a competitor were to suffer a major product glitch? Could you react with a campaign targeted at competitive customers? You probably wouldn't mention the glitch, but it would be nice to pop up just when customers are dealing with a headache. Maybe you could help them relieve the pain.

The same is true for regulatory issues. If you are in an industry with specific regulation requirements, changes to those requirements can be a challenge if you're not on top of it. What if the government changes a regulation requiring your category of products to include a specific new feature? If there is a delay between the time the new regulation goes into effect and the time when your product complies with the regulation - you'll have some explaining to do.

Social, political and economic factors also have a direct impact on how you market your products. As the price of gasoline continues to rise in the US, manufacturers of trucks and SUVs are finding it harder and harder to market around their "MPG" statistics. It is much easier for Toyota to market the Prius, or Saturn to market the Aura to a customer base that is sensitive to the increasing cost of gasoline. Not to mention the impact of environmental concerns like global-warming.

Things change over time, and your marketing needs to evolve to keep pace, to position you competitively, and to take into account of changing market conditions and customer needs. A good rule of thumb for marketing messages is that they typically have a lifespan of 12-18 months (depending on the industry). Some people freak out when I say this - remember I'm talking about messages, not copy (see Rule 34). Your copy can and should adapt frequently to reflect these changes. That doesn't mean you should change your underlying messages that often.

The core idea should stay consistent. The words you use to communicate with customers should connect with current industry trends, cultural or social happenings or topical political issues.

27 PR Doesn't Mean Press Release

PR professionals know that it takes a lot more to make news than a press release

PR usually stands for "public relations" or "press relations." It is an unfortunate coincidence that it also stands for one of the more visible elements of many marketing campaigns - a press release. Unfortunately, there are a lot of people who instinctively think that PR means "press release." They couldn't be more wrong.

In the olden days, news used to be sent out "over the wire" which actually meant a telegraph wire. Fortunately, we've moved beyond that. In the not so distant past, you just had to hire a PR agency that would subscribe to a "wire service," write your press releases and distribute news on your behalf. Once it went out over the wire it became news...ta da!

PR professionals know that it takes a lot more to make news than a press release. First, you have to have news. Yep - a real story that people will care about enough to pay attention. Adding a new feature to an existing product isn't news, unless you can connect it to something a customer did that they couldn't do before they had the feature. That becomes a story that other customers can relate to and the media might be willing to write about.

Speaking of the media, relationships are absolutely essential if you want to get your story told. There are a lot more media folks out there these days. By media I mean, journalists, bloggers, editors, product reviewers and such. Identifying the key players for your industry is crucial. In fact, you can have a major PR campaign with tremendous coverage without ever doing a press release. Politicians do this all the time. They have a story to tell, constituents who can help them tell it, and they have relationships with the local media. No press release needed.

PR has not been left out of the Internet revolution. In fact, the number of press releases has increased exponentially with the advent of online news distribution services like PRWeb. The combination of online news distribution and search engine optimization has expanded the role of traditional PR.

Press releases used to be the way to get your news to journalists. Today, press releases are delivered via RSS feeds to your customers' desktops. Press releases have become an indication of "market momentum" - at least that's what some people believe. Press releases have become another marketing tactic that, if used properly, can be effective. They are general purpose tools that work well if you're trying to make people aware that you exist. Press releases aren't particularly helpful if you need to generate leads.

Customers, journalists, bloggers and anyone else with a computer can check any number of online news sites and get more information than they know what to do with. As a result, journalists are less likely to react to press releases than they used to be. They are shifting to other sources for new story ideas and breaking news. Direct emails or phone calls are very effective if you have done your homework and invested the time necessary to create relationships.

EscapeHomes is an online marketplace for second homes. David Hehman, the President at the time, went to real estate conventions, met with journalists and the real estate trade association and made himself an invaluable source of information. When someone wanted a quote on the second home market, they went to David. He became the industry expert. And EscapeHomes became the go-to spot on the Internet for second homes.

The types of relationships David established with his target media are more important now than ever. Direct discussion with your target media is crucial. Make sure they know who you are. Send them little nuggets of information. Provide them with customers they can talk to and get quotes, anecdotes and background for their stories. Help a reporter do their job better and faster, and you will have a friend for life.

28 Tradeshows Will Never Die

Tradeshows and events are still a credible and viable element in any marketing mix

A lot of marketers think tradeshows are dead. Yet, seventy-two percent of US manufacturers plan to invest in Tradeshows/Events, according to MarketingSherpa's Business Technology Benchmark Guide 2006.[9] Now that almost everything can be done online or virtually, it is easy to assume that the tried and true industry tradeshows are less important.

Not true, according to Tradeshow Week's annual report of consumer show statistics, which measured an increase of almost 16 percent in 2006. That means that 16 percent more consumers attended shows like the well-known Consumer Electronics Show as well as niche shows like Design Automation Conference, Wizard World, and SuperZoo (I didn't make that one up, I swear). These shows are still very product focused. Potential customers can see, touch, hear and even taste the products they are interested in.

You can't get that kind of experience online or in a virtual tradeshow. Yep - virtual tradeshows are a concept being tested by several online companies. For example, eComXpo is a virtual tradeshow for interactive, online marketers. The show is completely virtual; which makes sense since their entire industry is focused on virtual experiences. For more traditional industries, the idea might not fly.

Like other marketing tactics, Tradeshows need to be part of your overall plan. You need to know what you're trying to accomplish by participating in the show - what is the objective? If you're trying to increase awareness and generate leads then Tradeshows are a great vehicle. If you're trying to convert leads to sales then Tradeshows are not the best choice.

A popular trend these days is to structure "events within an event." These events are more about building relationships with customers, suppliers and partners (sound familiar?). Many companies are using the tradeshow venue to meet with customers and to do in-person product demonstrations, simulations or other experiential activities that you just can't do online.

Smaller vertical trade events and niche conferences are becoming more popular because they tend to produce more qualified leads - 25 percent more according to a MarketingSherpa study. In general or broad-based events, the qualified lead ratio was 27.6 percent whereas the vertical events had a qualified lead ratio of 40.7 percent.[10] Pretty good uplift, I'd say.

Another benefit to participating in vertical events is the relative ease with which you can engage in multiple aspects of the show. In fact, you can almost "own" these shows if you want to. Marketing Transformation Services (MTS) is a boutique consulting firm specializing in marketing resource management (MRM) strategy and implementation. The principal, Beth Weesner, is very well-known in MRM circles because of how she leveraged a semi-annual vertical event - the Henry Stewart Marketing Operations Management Symposium. Ms. Weesner gave the keynote address and hosted a panel discussion. Several of her clients were featured speakers. She hosted an invitation-only cocktail reception for existing and potential clients. Pre and post-event marketing was negotiated with the event managers to build on success of the event. The leads generated from these events fill the MTS pipeline and keep the name visible between events.

Tradeshows and events are still a credible and viable element in any marketing mix. Whether they are small vertical trade events, in-house user groups or general business conferences, they are here to stay.

29 Clicks Aren't Customers

Gauging effectiveness doesn't need to be complicated and overly engineered

Without clear objectives, how do you know if you were successful? If you didn't define what success looked like up front - how do you know if your plan worked? It's good to be flexible, to try new things and see what happens - some of the most creative inventions of our time happened that way. But for most of us, most of the time, it's a good idea to know what you're aiming for.

In order to evaluate the effectiveness of any type of campaign (online or offline) you have to be able to measure the impact it had on a defined criteria. The measurement could be click through on your website, calls to a 1-800 number, or actual sales volume and revenue targets. Gauging effectiveness doesn't need to be complicated and overly engineered. Some of the most sophisticated analytical models work because they are very simple. Let's take a basic online campaign and do the math.

Assume conversion rates on websites today are about 1-3 percent (meaning about 1-3 percent of clicks turn into customers). Let's say you did an online ad campaign for $5000. The campaign generated an incremental 2500 visits to your site (we know that because you can track against average daily traffic for similar days prior to the campaign). The results of the campaign (affectionately known as return on investment or ROI) would look like this:

Cost	$5,000
Increased traffic	2500 visits
Cost per visit	$2.00
Conversion rate	3% (being generous)
Actual customers	75
Cost per customer	$66.67

This means that in order for the campaign to break even each customer must purchase at least $66.67 worth of stuff as a result of your campaign. Looking at it a different way, it cost you $66.67 to get each new customer.

Depending on your business, this may be good - it may even be great. You'll never know unless you do the math and have a target to measure your results against. Cost per acquisition, or CPA, is a common metric used to track return on investment for this type of online campaign.

For the data to make sense, you need to track enough campaign data to give you some directional guidance. In this example, a campaign is defined as an email with a unique subject, offer and call-to-action. If you executed 30 individual email campaigns you would end up with enough data to develop a benchmark for measuring the success of future campaigns. Once you know your target CPA you have a very clear objective.

This type of model helps you evaluate and prioritize your investments. You'll definitely know when it works and when it doesn't.

A Launch is a Process, Not an Event

Planning your launch so that each activity is integrated with the next takes teamwork, organization and patience

One of the biggest challenges for marketers is "the launch." Whether it is the initial company launch, the launch of a second-generation product, or a launch into a new market segment - the process is similar and the results are equally important.

"Launch" is one of those tricky marketing words. If you ask three people for a definition, you will get three different answers. I define launch as the beginning of an overall integrated marketing campaign. When a launch is planned as a stand-alone event - a big party with industry press, analysts and customers - you will usually see a spike in press coverage. That spike will generate awareness and demand, which leads to initial sales. But then it tends to flattens out. This is when people start to second-guess their revenue forecasts. Sales starts to question whether Marketing is doing its job. Marketing starts to question why Sales can't close the deals.

Every launch has a beginning, a middle, and an end. If planned well, one launch will lead right into the next. A launch can take many different forms. It can be a "big bang" or "crescendo" where activities lead up to or are triggered by a specific event. It can be more like "rolling thunder" where activities are happening over a period of time. The key here is that a launch is not an event. It is a series of related marketing activities focused around a single purpose - achieving your business objective.

Planning your launch so that each activity is integrated with the next takes teamwork, organization and patience. I like to start by picking a launch date - you have to start somewhere. Remember the launch isn't an event, but it is always helpful to have a deadline (see Rule 37.) The date can be tied to an industry event, a holiday or season, or basic product availability.

Once you have your deadline, the launch date, you can begin to develop a launch plan by working backwards. List all the activities you have planned for the launch. Identify the dependencies. For example, you need creative content from the landing page to include in the email campaign; you need the messaging before you create the datasheet; you need a customer testimonial for the website and the sales presentation. Based on the timing of each activity, create a timeline of when each item is due, and who is responsible for getting it done.

Your plan should have three main sections. First, activities leading up to the launch date like developing the messaging, creating the webpage, sales presentation and datasheet. Second, specific activities that occur on the day of the launch like when and how the website goes live, the email campaign begins, the press release is issued. Finally, activities to continue the excitement like feature articles, customer webinars, sales contests, email and viral campaigns.

Steve Larsen, CEO of Krugle, used participation in the DEMO conference as one element of his plan to launch Krugle in 2006. Larsen's goal for DEMO was to get 1-2,000 users signed-up for the beta product. Three days after the conference, Krugle has signed up 35,000 users. The follow-up communications became a critical element in Krugle's marketing plan. The event was only the beginning. The real work had just started.

Your launch plan doesn't have to be complicated. It does need to be a living launch plan. Things have a way of changing. You need to be able to adjust quickly as you learn more, and identify the impact of changes on other activities. Having everything written down helps you identify the impact of changes across all elements of the launch.

It also helps minimize the "oops" factor - that tiny little detail that falls through the cracks, and that your boss and colleagues will remind you about for years to come.

31 Don't Get Caught in the Hype

Hip, cool, trendy activities are fun to create, plan and execute — But they don't work for everyone

You have an exciting strategy; your messages are relevant and integrated throughout all customer interactions. Now you need an actionable marketing plan that delivers your message to your customers in ways that will increase the chance that they will pay attention, and ultimately purchase something from you.

Hip, cool, trendy activities are fun to create, plan and execute. But they don't work for everyone. But sometimes you don't know unless you try. Go ahead and try new things. Be bold. Let your "freak flag fly" (so to speak). But do so with a purpose.

It is easy to get excited about the latest technology or cool marketing technique. Street marketing, viral videos, user-generated advertising - are all very fun to create if you're a marketer. But you have to remember that the end result is to sell more stuff. If a cool new viral tactic is appealing to your target audience, then go for it. If your target audience is less technically savvy and wouldn't know YouTube from a "boob tube" then you should probably pick a different tactic.

You don't need to do everything in order to be effective. You do need to strategically select a few key activities and do them exceptionally well. A few well-executed tactics will produce better results than a whole slew of mediocre ones.

Just because it is inexpensive and easy to create your own website, doesn't mean you have to make it big and complex. Sometimes a smaller, well-written and well-structured site is much more effective than a site that "looks big" but is full of useless, complicated or unintelligible information.

Just because everyone and their dog happens to have a blog today doesn't mean that everyone and their dog should have a blog. Blogs are a great way to get your content picked up by search engines. Depending on what you're trying to do, a blog can be very effective. But they aren't a cure-all for poor search engine marketing.

Just because a few well-known companies have used viral marketing to build their customer base doesn't mean that it works for everyone. These companies are the outliers, the exceptions. That's why they are so well known. Not every campaign is "The Blair Witch Project."[11] Not all email footers will have the same impact Hotmail had.[12] What about the companies that tried the same approach only to have their products smashed to bits in the blogosphere, never to be heard from again?

One marketing tactic does not equal a strategy (see Rule 23). It takes a combination of tactics to execute a strategy. Using a range of tactics helps to surround your customers with messages in a lot of ways, increasing the likelihood that the message is received.

Focusing on the quality of your marketing, not the quantity of your campaigns will ultimately drive results. Quality is measured by how relevant your message is to your customers, and how effectively the message is delivered. In the end, your customers will tell you if your campaigns are working.

32 The Whole is Greater Than the Sum of its Parts

Integrated marketing is about combining multiple marketing elements together to achieve an objective more efficiently and effectively than by implementing any one element alone

You are bombarded with thousands of messages each day - personally and professionally. Some say it's the Internet; some say it's all the new media channels the Internet has enabled. Whatever the cause, the effect is the same. The volume of marketing messages is overwhelming to most Americans. In fact, overwhelming numbers of people have signed up for the do-not-call registry; almost everyone I know has installed Web pop-up blockers; there is even a do-not-email list. So the question is: "How do you break through in this environment?" One answer: integrated marketing.

Integrated marketing is about combining multiple marketing elements together to achieve an objective more efficiently and effectively than by implementing any one element alone. It is the case where 1+1 really does equal 3; where the whole is greater than the sum of its parts.

$$1 + 1 = 3$$

Independent marketing tactics like PR, events, or email marketing tactics do little to attract customers and drive revenue in and of themselves. However, when these activities are combined as part of an integrated marketing strategy, these and other tactics are the foundation of a marketing plan that will deliver results. Sounds simple, right? Well, often the simplest things are the hardest to do.

Think of it as a stage production. Each performer knows their role. They know when they are supposed to go on stage and what they are supposed to do. It is the same with integrated marketing campaigns. Each person who is responsible for creating an element of the campaign - the PR manager, the graphic design, or the webmaster - should know how they fit into the overall production.

This type of orchestration helps the production flow smoothly. The audience enjoys the show because it is organized, energetic and delivered flawlessly. The result is a performance the audience will remember.

You want your audience, your customers, to enjoy the production. You want them to remember your company, and your message. That in turn drives them to consider your product when they are in purchase mode. When you integrate your messages and your tactics the effect is like seeing U2 or The Police live on-stage. Unforgettable.

33 Marketing Plans are Good

Please don't confuse your marketing plan with a long list of tactics

Every business must have a marketing plan. It can be a simple one-page email sent around the office or it can be a more complex document that includes stats, references or external reports. Whatever form it takes, you must have one.

During a presentation to the Silicon Valley Product Management Association, Mark Hammit, of Crossbridge Consulting said "marketing plans establish a clear understanding of the resources marketing requires in order to commit to a specific revenue forecast. If you give me resources, then I can commit to deliver the corresponding revenue."

Your marketing plan helps you formulate your ideas so you can identity the right kinds of messages and activities. It helps you allocate budget to your specific marketing activities. PR gets this much, direct marketing gets this much, and customer events get the rest. Regardless of the type or size of your business, having a committed marketing budget is one of the fundamental requirements of success.

Your marketing plan also helps rally people around the same goal. It improves communication, because everyone has a clear understanding of what you're doing and why. It helps make your plans better. It is easier for people to respond to something that is written down - they see things that are missing, redundant, overlap and so on. The result is a better plan, and people who are more committed to it, because they were part of the process of creating it.

An unintended consequence of creating a marketing plan is that you actually increase/improve creativity. For example, you're attending a tradeshow and have planned a customer appreciation cocktail reception. The PR or direct marketing people might look at that as an opportunity to create some viral buzz by making it an "invitation-only" event and secretly handing out invites to people at the event. This adds a "cool" factor and creates its own kind of viral marketing within the show - your party is the place to be. Awareness of your company goes way up. Assuming the tradeshow is well positioned towards your target customer - that's a good thing.

To be helpful, your marketing plan must address six key ideas:

1. What are you trying to accomplish? (Objective/Goal)
2. Who are you trying to reach? (Target Customers)
3. How will you go about achieving your goals? (Strategy)
4. What specific activities are you going to invest in? (Tactics)
5. When will you do each activity? (Timeline)
6. How much are you going to spend? (Budget)

The following would do just fine for a smaller company: "We will increase revenue by offering our existing customer base preferred product ordering and support status. We will spend $5,000 to create an email marketing system in Q4 and deliver our first email campaign, combined with an initial investment in pay-per-click advertising." It covers the six ideas without being overwhelming. Not all marketing plans can be this simplistic. But they shouldn't be a 150-page Power-Point presentation either.

Please don't confuse your marketing plan with a long list of tactics. The plan will contain the tactics, but it must also contain the reasons for them. Remember, it doesn't have to be complicated to be effective. Find the right balance and make it work for you, not the other way around.

NOTE Check out the Marketing Plan Template at www.lauralowell.com/products.

34 Marketing is Art

Art is emotional and marketing is art; therefore marketing must be emotional in order to be effective

There was a time when marketing, and advertising especially, was more about the creative ideas than the business impact they delivered. SuperBowl advertising[13] is probably one of the best known examples of this phenomenon. Many of these ads are art for the sake of art. They don't connect to the company, brand or product. Sometimes they don't even make sense...but they are usually brilliantly creative works of art.

In fact, marketing shouldn't be art for the sake of art. It should be about using the art to help you accomplish your business objective, and using the art to connect with people emotionally.

The art is visual. It tells you who the company is; how the product works; and what the brand stands for. They say "a picture is worth 1,000 words." With marketing, sometimes all you have is pictures. You have to learn how to use pictures to tell your story.

The art is also partly about the use of language. You also have to learn how to tell your story in a new and different way; to connect the pictures to your company and your customers.

Unilever tried a rather risky strategy when they released the "Real Beauty" campaign featuring "normal-sized" women. The campaign featured images of regular women in their underwear. Unilever used a combination of tactics including print and broadcast advertising, and viral marketing that asked people to help define "real beauty." The campaign was very successful and caused a significant increase is sales of Dove products. Even more impressive was the positive and negative reactions the campaign evoked from both men and women.

The images evoked very powerful emotional reactions either way. It seemed as thought people either loved or hated the campaign. The women were either "fat" or "fabulous." The marketing strategy was to focus the reaction and get people talking about what real beauty was - to connect with Dove customers about something that was important to them.

The emotional connection is where the art starts. Don't be afraid of emotion in marketing. Art is emotional and marketing is art; therefore marketing must be emotional in order to be effective.

The magic occurs when you can use the art to inspire, and to evoke a strong emotional reaction from your customers. Like all art, it is about images, words and emotions.

35 Marketing is Science

One of the most important measures of a successful marketing campaign is the impact on sales

Never launch a campaign without a way to measure its performance. The first question anyone will ask is "How's it going?" Unless you have identified metrics, you really don't have a good answer except "Pretty good, thanks."

Measurement needs to be part of the entire campaign creation process. Upfront, when you're trying to identify the campaign message or theme, it is important to do some level of market research so you can validate your ideas and make sure they work for the audience. Then you need to test your specific campaign copy and creative images to make sure they have the impact you intended.

I once did a campaign test for a consumer technology product in China. We expected them to love the technology and hate the images we used to describe it since we had not localized the images enough for the Chinese market (or so we thought). In fact, they loved the images (they were hip and cool), but they didn't get the technology at all. In the end it turned out that we used the images in conjunction with more descriptive copy, and it worked great. But we never would have known if we hadn't done the test.

In some cases there are infrastructure requirements in order to be able to track and report the results. If this isn't in place before you "hit the send button," you might not be able to track and report on all of your campaign activities.

Once you have tested your campaign, you're confident that it is working towards your objectives, and you have the infrastructure in place to measure the result - you're ready to go. Each type of marketing activity has a set of performance metrics used to gauge effectiveness. Email marketing uses open rates, click-through and conversion rates - did they do what I wanted them to do? Tradeshows and events look at attendance rates, lead capture and follow-up rates.

Once the campaign is live, is when the fun begins. You get to see responses real-time in some cases; who is responding, what they are responding to, and what actions they are taking. This information can be used to "tweak" the campaign and improve performance.

MerchantCircle, a start-up in the local online advertising business, has mastered this. They are pretty diligent about testing email subject lines, for example. They have found that emails with "get more customers" in the headline work really well for their members as well as potential members. When they want to launch a new campaign, they test a few headlines and see how they perform. They take that information and create the actual email subject line that goes to customers. Then, as the campaign goes live, they watch how it does and apply whatever they learn to the next campaign and so on. While it is common sense, it isn't commonly practiced by some marketing teams.

One of the most important measures of a successful marketing campaign is the impact on sales. Sales can be tracked by revenue (obviously). You can track sales results on actual campaign performance like the number of products purchased online as a result of the campaign. Or you can use the number of qualified leads provided to your sales force and apply a "conversion to sales ratio," which is a historical calculation that indicates the rate at which sales closes deals.

What you track isn't as important as how and when you track it. Consistently being able to show the results of your activities is critical to the overall perception of marketing as a revenue center, as opposed to a cost center.

36 Make Them Laugh

The key to using humor in marketing is to make sure it is in context and has some relevant connection to your audience

Don't take your company, your product, or yourself too seriously. Humor is one of the most effective ways to connect with individuals. And, regardless of what some large enterprise companies might have you believe, CIOs are people too.

There is a commonly-held belief that in order to be credible with a big established company like State Farm, Fidelity or GM you need to be really traditional, conservative and respectable. In other words, you have to be boring. I'm not sure where this belief springs from, but I think it's crazy!

Their target customers get nothing but serious messages all day long. A little humor would stand out and maybe prompt a chuckle. Aha, you're in...now you have established a nice sub-conscious connection with the person. You might have brightened an otherwise dreary day, or given them a little shot in the arm right when they needed it. The fact is, you've connected on a different level than the companies talking about "scalability, reliability and availability."

What is traditionally thought of as "business to business" marketing is really "business to business person" marketing. Ultimately you are talking to people, not other companies. People do research. People make recommendations. People make decisions.

CIOs (to continue with the example) are smart. They can tell the difference between something intended to get their attention, like an ad, and something intended to give them information, like a white paper. Even if the subject is serious, they know it is serious. They don't need you to remind them over and over again. Acknowledge the serious side of the business issue. But it doesn't mean you have to make your marketing serious too.

Some of our "b-to-b" colleagues could take a lesson from the "business to consumer" handbook. Humor is more the norm in consumer marketing. For a quick study course on humor in marketing, check out www.veryfunnyads.com - a collection of ads from all over the world. You can see everything from kids playing with vibrators (IKEA France) to men racing cheetahs (Charal) to the effects of defective merchandise on an unsuspecting fellow trying to get a workout (Citibank).

Humor can take many forms - visual, verbal, or written. It can come from many places - current events, personal life, or public personalities. The key to using humor in marketing is to make sure it is in context and has some relevant connection to your audience. A CIO might not get a joke about the latest episode of the WB series All of Us. But they probably would get a reference to Fox's 24 or HBO's The Sopranos.

Humor is just like other marketing messages. It needs to be targeted to your audience. It needs to help you tell your story in a way that will get their attention. It needs to connect with them on a different level so they remember something special about your company or your product. There's nothing funny about that.

37 Always Have a Deadline

As helpful as deadlines are to get things started, they also have an additional benefit — Deadlines give you a point to stop

Almost everyone does better work when faced with a deadline. Deadlines create a sense of urgency; a perception of immediacy. Deadlines give you a place to start. The date can be based on market timing, industry trends, or seasonality. However you came by the deadline, it gives you a timeline to work from and your team a goal to work towards.

With a deadline established, you can start with the end in mind and begin planning your activities. If you figure out what needs to happen, then you can work backwards to define the specific steps in priority order that have to be accomplished to achieve the end results.

You can have deadlines within deadlines if you need to. The deadline for one activity becomes the beginning of the next activity. For example, you need to have the product manual completed before you can figure out your printing strategy and approach to what goes into the product package. So the product manual people have a deadline to deliver their material to the packaging people. The packaging folks need to have the packaging costs worked out so that the finance people can do the math and figure out product margins and establish pricing guidelines. And so on, and so on…

Deadlines also provide a level of accountability: internally to yourself, and externally to your team. You can commit to yourself to manage to a certain schedule based on the final deadline. Your team knows what they have to accomplish in order to meet their deadline.

Think about a product launch. In order to launch a product in the Fall as part of a "Back to School" campaign, you need product information several months ahead of time so that you can develop the messaging, the campaign copy and the creative images necessary to launch. You can't really begin developing the campaign until the content is created (messaging, copy and images). Your team knows who needs what type of information from them. They are accountable to provide the information so the rest of the project can move forward.

As helpful as deadlines are to get things started, they also have an additional benefit. Deadlines give you a point to stop. There is a tendency to continually edit, revise, and improve your work. At some point, you begin to experience diminishing returns. The incremental improvements are not worth the delay in schedule. You have to stop. The product must ship, the campaign must go live, or the company must launch.

Jason Feinsmith, CEO of Accomplice Software, leveraged a very well-known launch event for start-ups, the DEMO conference. Being a part of DEMO pushed the limits of the company and the team. It set clear deadlines for publicly unveiling the product and for stopping product development in order to begin building the demo. While DEMO is a very specific event, the plans Feinsmith put in place leading up to and after the event were significant.

You have probably committed to certain business goals. If you don't launch your company, or your product, or your campaign, then you won't be able to deliver against your commitment. As the saying goes, "If it wasn't for the last minute, nothing would ever get done."

38 Everyone is a Marketing Expert

Everyone might have an opinion, but in the end you're the one that gets to decide how you do your job

When you are a marketer, everyone thinks they can do your job better than you. Everyone from your spouse, friends, colleague and even the folks at your local coffee shop - they all have opinions on your latest marketing campaign. "I would have..." "Why didn't you...?" "I don't get it."

What other professions can you think of where everyone gets to tell you how to do your job? You don't tell the engineers how to solve technical problems. You don't tell doctors how to diagnose an illness. You wouldn't tell a lawyer how to prosecute their case. Yet engineers, doctors and lawyers feel like they can tell how you should have done your latest TV ad.

I used to work for a General Manager who was pretty well-known for asking the marketing team "How hard can it be?" After trying to explain the issues and challenges, we finally resorted to a rather unexpected response, "It's pretty @#$%^ hard." After staring at us in disbelief at the response, he was able to listen to our recommendations and understand what we were doing and why. He was able to let us do our job.

Marketing is not something that can be done by consensus. It is very useful to have lots of input and opinions during the initial brainstorming phases of a campaign. At that point, the more ideas you have, the better off you are. It is great to test your ideas with people who are not as close to the project as you are. It's even fun to describe what you're doing at a cocktail party and see how people react.

The part that most people don't understand is that their ideas and opinions actually have to make sense with the overall marketing strategy and your business objectives. Even though your colleague's wife might have a really creative idea at the company BBQ - if it doesn't help you achieve your goals then it isn't helpful, no matter how creative it is.

The folks providing you their "expert" opinions don't have all the information you have. They don't understand the history, they can't see the bigger picture and they don't know the market dynamics you might be facing. So you should cut them a little slack. After all, they are usually just trying to be helpful.

Everyone might have an opinion, but in the end you're the one that gets to decide how you do your job. With that said, you should be polite; at least to a point. You should listen to what they have to say and try to keep an open mind on the rare chance that they might actually have a good idea.

When the idea is just silly, you smile, nod and say "Thanks for the input." Then do whatever you darn well please.

39 Deliver What You Promise

There is nothing wrong with creating an environment of anticipation — But the experience better pay off

There is a classic holiday movie that my family watches every year after Thanksgiving dinner - A Christmas Story.

Set in the 1940s, the movie is about a young boy, Ralphie, his mother, father and little brother. There are a dozen memorable scenes in the movie. Ralphie's friend gets his tongue stuck on a lamp post in the dead of winter after another friend "double dog dares" him to try it. Ralphie asks his mother for a "Red Rider BB gun" for Christmas to which she replies "You're gonna shoot your eye out."

There is one scene that is especially relevant for marketers. Ralphie and his brother are big fans of the "Little Orphan Annie" radio hour. As part of a promotion, the listeners were encouraged to send away for the secret decoder ring, and they would receive a secret message from Annie herself.

Ralphie could hardly stand it. He ran home from school everyday to check the mail, only to be disappointed. Then finally, one day, there was a large envelope addressed to him. It must be his decoder ring. He could hardly wait. He ran straight into the house and locked himself in the bathroom. He sat down and began to decode the secret message from Annie herself.

Letter by painstaking letter, the message appeared. He couldn't work fast enough. He had to know what Little Orphan Annie wanted to tell him. D.....R.....I....oh, the anticipation. N....K....come on. M....O...R....E...O...V...A...L...T...I...N...E.

You have got to be kidding! "Drink more Ovaltine." Ralphie was crushed. He threw down the decoder ring and never felt quite the same about Ovaltine or Little Orphan Annie.

The lesson I've always taken away from that scene is that it is your responsibility as a marketer to deliver what you promise.

There is nothing wrong with creating an environment of anticipation. It is a great strategy and can pay off big time. But the experience better pay off. Otherwise it can backfire big time.

What about poor Ralphie? The makers of Ovaltine sponsored the Little Orphan Annie radio hour in order to sell more of their product. Unfortunately their promotion had the opposite effect. It alienated a poor little kid and probably turned him off Ovaltine forever. Not exactly good for business.

40 Give it a Chance

When you change your message or creative images or branding before the campaign has had a chance to sink in, you are wasting the investment in the campaign

Good marketers have patience. Studies show that it takes anywhere from five to nine exposures for a customers to recognize a marketing message. And that only means that they recognize it as a message - not that they identify it with your company or product.

In order for your marketing to "sink in" customers need to be exposed to your message over and over again. Repeated exposure leads to awareness that the message comes from you. Think about some of the really engaging ads on TV or radio. How many times have you heard people say "I love that commercial, but I can't remember who the company is." This is not what you want to hear.

Creating an integrated marketing plan is one of the best ways to build up these repeated exposures. Not only do your customers need to see your messages over and over again, but they need to see them in different places. The right mix of activities touches your customers at different times and connects with them in different ways.

An email, a phone call, a presence at a tradeshow, partnerships with other companies, editorial articles in trade or business magazines

- all reach your customers when they are in different places thinking different thoughts. At some point, the message will be more relevant and in the right context, and will cause the message to sink in.

Managing your campaigns is much like planting a garden. You find the perfect spot to plant your garden. You prepare the soil, plant the seeds and water and care for them until they finally sprout. Then you have to make sure they get enough sunlight and water, and you have to try to keep the bugs at bay. Then, after patiently caring for them, you walk out one morning, and the garden is in full bloom.

Unfortunately for some, the campaigns are changed before they have a chance to bloom. The ideas for the change can come from over-eager executives, agencies or even your team. The team works really hard on the campaign, and it might take you three weeks or three months to get your campaign to market.

If it takes you that long to create the campaign, it will probably take at least that long for your customers to recognize it and connect it to your company or product. When you change your message or creative images or branding before the campaign has had a chance to sink in, you are wasting the investment in the campaign. The time, energy and money used to create the campaign aren't allowed to grow and have the desired impact.

If you change too early or too often, you never build a foundation of awareness. You continually have to start from scratch (preparing the soil, planting the seeds, etc.) This costs more and delivers less.

It takes a strong constitution to stand up to the pressures you might feel to "change things up" before your campaign has truly proved itself. You should always learn as you go and refine your copy and your offers as you go. But leave the core messages, images and tone of the campaign intact.

Once they sink in you will have a foundation to build from. Have a little patience, and give your campaign a chance to grow.

Don't Follow the Pack

Just because one approach worked for a competitor doesn't mean it will work for you

Just because a specific strategy works for one company doesn't mean it will work for you. You need to find the right mix of messages and marketing tactics to connect with your customers. It is tempting to copy effective marketing strategies. After all, if it worked for them, it should work for you, right? Not always.

Strategies must connect to your objectives and be relevant to your company, your product and your brand. It would seem odd and inconsistent for a company like Northwestern Mutual to use street marketing to promote a new commercial insurance plan. How would it feel to see Lucky Jeans advertising on website targeting adults over 55? These are dramatic examples, but you get my point.

Your strategies and tactics must be authentic. It must "feel right" to your customers to hear a specific message from your company and see your messages in certain venues.

A study commissioned by Gartner Group and Insight Express[14] found that business leaders spend more time on the Web than they do with any other media. "The Web has evolved to be the most important business information resource" according to the study. In fact, 67 percent of the

C-level executives surveyed said they considered the Internet the most important source of business information. The next closest was newspapers at 16 percent.

But what about consumers? A study by the Pew Internet & American Life Project[15], identified 31 percent of American consumers as "Elite Tech Users." These folks are heavy and frequent users of the Internet and technology in general.

The Internet is an important and effective marketing tactic for both business and consumer audiences. This is what I'd call a "blinding glimpse of the obvious." Yet using an Internet strategy that worked for a consumer audience to deliver a message to a business audience probably isn't the most effective approach.

Viral marketing worked for MySpace and YouTube, but it didn't happen overnight as most people think. MySpace was launched late in 2003 and wasn't an "overnight success" until it was acquired by Fox in 2005. In the meantime, MySpace leveraged online viral emails, but ultimately found that offline tactics like sponsoring parties at clubs, with bands and promoters, worked better at growing the community. MySpace also had access to a major distribution partner in Intermix (who actually owned MySpace). They were able to leverage the media buying power of Intermix to increase their visibility and ad revenues. It was the overall marketing strategy that enabled MySpace to be so successful. Plus, they had an idea that was easy to understand, simple to use and just plain fun.

Researching different methods and activities and benchmarking what the competition is doing is very important. It helps you put your activities in context and positions your activities and messages accordingly.

However, just because one approach worked for a competitor doesn't mean it will work for you. If your colleagues decide to jump off a cliff, it doesn't mean that you have to.

42

These are My Rules.
What are Yours?

Resources

**Interesting
Things to Read
and Do**

I came across of lot of really cool stuff while doing research for this book. I found some interesting, fun, quirky and helpful resources that I'd like to share with you.

If you have other resources you'd like to share, please let me know at laura@impact-mg.com.

Bullfighter: Bullfighter is the epoch-defining software that works with Microsoft Word and PowerPoint to help you find and eliminate jargon in your documents. It may look like a little toolbar with three buttons, but it's actually much more. Bullfighter includes a jargon database and an exclusive Bull Composite Index calculator that will allow you to see -- in an actual window, on your PC display, live -- just how bad a document can be. Bullfighter is freeware originally produced by Deloitte Consulting, now available as a standalone product. Source: http://www.fightthebull.com/bullfighter.asp

Pew Internet and American Life Project: The Pew Internet & American Life Project produces reports that explore the impact of the Internet on families, communities, work and home, daily life, education, health care, and civic and political life. The project aims to be an authoritative source on the evolution of the Internet through collection of data and analysis of real-world developments as they affect the virtual world. Source: http://www.pewInternet.org/reports.asp

MarketingSherpa: MarketingSherpa is a research firm specializing in tracking what works in all aspects of marketing (and what does not.) Source: http://www.marketingsherpa.com

eMarketer: eMarketer is "The First Place to Look" for market research and trend analysis on Internet, e-business, online marketing, media and emerging technologies. eMarketer aggregates and analyzes information from over 2,800 sources, and brings it together in analyst reports, daily research articles and the most comprehensive database of e-business and online marketing statistics in the world. Source: http://www.emarketer.com

Online Journalism Review: As part of the University of Southern California's Annenberg School for Communication and funded by USC's Annenberg Center for Education, our mission is the development and continuing education of professional online journalists. Source: http://www.ojr.org/

VeryFunnyAds.com: Source: http://www.veryfunnyads.com

Moon Ray: MoonRay software offers a host of different features from enterprise-level email management, multi-channel marketing process automation and rule-based triggers, to ROI tracking and testing. Source: http://www.moon-ray.com

The Krugle Case Study: Don Thorson was the VP of Marketing at Krugle and was responsible for launching the company at DEMO06. He describes his experience on his blog. Source: http://donthorson.typepad.com/don_thorson/krugle/index.html

Appendix

B References

Bibliography

1. To learn more about the Ultimate Answer to Life, The Universe and Everything you can check out the entry in Wikipedia at http://en.wikipedia.org/wiki/The_Answer_to_Life%2C_the_Universe%2C_and_Everything.

2. Wikipedia, E http://en.wikipedia.org/wiki/Demographics

3. Wikipedia, http://en.wikipedia.org/wiki/Psychographics

4. Wikipedia, http://en.wikipedia.org/wiki/Behavioral_targeting

5. Better, faster, cheaper" as coined by Daniel Saul Goldin who served as Administrator of NASA from 1992 to 2001 and pioneered the "faster, better, cheaper" approach that enabled NASA to cut costs while still delivering a wide variety of aerospace programs.

6. BullFighter, created by Deloitte Consulting and subsequently sold to Business Idiots, LLC and available online at http://www.fightthebull.com

7. Responsys, Inc. White Paper: 10 Quick Wins for Email Marketing

8. Lori Grant, SmartLemming.com, December 18th, 2006

9. Business Technology Benchmark Guide, 2006, MarketingSherpa

10. Business Technology Benchmark Guide, 2006, MarketingSherpa

11. The Blair Witch Project is described in detail at http://www.blairwitch.com/.

12. BusinessWeek, Viral Marketing Alert! by Ellen Neuborne, March 19, 2001.

13. http://www.superbowl-ads.com/2007/index.html

14. GartnerG2/Insight Express C-Level Study, September 2006 as referenced on Forbes.com

15. Pew Internet, & American Life Project

42 Rules Toolkit

The templates referenced in this book, and other more specialized marketing Toolkits are available for purchase at:
www.lauralowell.com/products

42 Rules Toolkit

As featured in the book, the 42 following marketing templates have been used by hundreds of professionals to help them improve the effectiveness of their marketing activities. The kit includes the following:

- Marketing Plan
- Launch Plan
- Target Audience Profile - Consumer and Business
- Message Development
- Message Testing
- Marketing Mix

The Big Launch Toolkit

For product managers, marcom managers, PR managers or entrepreneurs looking to launch a company or product, the Big Launch Toolkit has everything you need to be heard! The kit includes all the material in the Strategic Marketing Toolkit plus:

42 Rules of Marketing

- Marketing Plan
- Target Audience Profile - Consumer
- Target Audience Profile - Business
- Competitive Overview
- Positioning Worksheet
- Message Development
- Message Testing
- Launch Checklist
- Planning Calendar
- Planning Checklist
- Datasheet
- Press Release - Product
- Press Release - Customer/Partner
- Campaign Checklists
- Media Coverage Report
- Web page content template

The Strategic Marketing Toolkit

For business owners and senior managers looking to guide their teams, or individuals who want to be more impactful, this is a must-have Toolkit!

- Marketing Plan
- Target Audience Profile - Consumer
- Target Audience Profile - Business
- Competitive Overview
- Positioning Worksheet
- Message Development
- Message Testing
- Planning Calendar & Checklist

The PR Toolkit

For product managers, marcom managers, PR managers or entrepreneurs who need access to best-in-class models for creating press releases that generate coverage and buzz. This includes:

- PR Calendar
- Competitive Overview
- Media Coverage Report
- Press Release - Product
- Press Release - Customer/Partner

About the Author

Laura Lowell is passionate about helping companies be heard; to get the right message to the right customer at the right time. As a sought after consultant, author, and speaker in Silicon Valley, Laura has shared her pragmatic approach to marketing with hundreds of individuals and companies. Her work on the "client-side" has shaped her approach to marketing. She appreciates what it takes to get things done - in both start-ups and established companies.

Prior to launching Impact Marketing Group, Laura was the Director of Worldwide Consumer Marketing Communications for Hewlett-Packard where she was responsible for planning and implementing integrated marketing campaigns across all HP consumer product lines. Early in her career, Laura spent several years at Intel Corporation where she was on the start-up team that developed and implemented the Intel Inside® branding program.

Laura's degree in International Relations prepared her for work assignments in Hong Kong and London, after which she received her MBA from UC Berkeley's Haas School of Business, with an emphasis on marketing and entrepreneurship. She lives in Los Gatos, California, with her husband Rick, their two daughters, and their dog.

Write Your Own Rules

Published by Super Star Press, the 42 Rules book series is composed of books focused on a single topic that condense the fundamental elements of that topic into 42 simple rules.

The books are practical reminders of things you know you should do, but don't. They are fun, easy-to-read chapteres and use real life examples to make the point. '42 Rules of Marketing' is the first book in the series. Upcoming titles include 42 Rules of ... finding the perfect job, parenting, adoption, selling your house and a lot more.

Write a book

The author of an entire book will receive 250 copies of the book and a professionally created marketing plan, plus ongoing coaching assistance from Laura Lowell as the executive editor of the series.

Cost: $4500

Write a rule

The contributor of a rule(s) to a compilation book will receive 100 copies of the book and the contributor's name will be listed next to the rule and in the "about the authors" section of the book, as well as on the 42 Rules web site. Promotional opportunities as part of the 42 Rules series are available for a fee.

Cost: $750 per rule

Start writing your rules...contact:

Super Star Press, 408-257-3000
E-mail: info@superstarpress.com

Why Write Today?

Books deliver instant credibility to the author. Having an MBA or PhD is great, however, putting the word "author" in front of your name is similar to using the letters PHD or MBA. You are no long Michael Green, you are "Author Michael Green."

Books give you a platform to stand on. They help you to:

- Demonstrate your thought leadership
- Generate leads

Books deliver increased revenue, particularly indirect revenue

- A typical consultant will make 3x in indirect revenue for every dollar they make on book sales

Books are better than a business card. They are:

- More powerful than white papers
- An item that makes it to the book shelf vs. the circular file
- The best tschocke you can give at a conference

Other Happy About Books

Is it who or what one knows that makes the difference? Both!

'Tales From The Networking Community' gives you tips, techniques and shares anecdotal stories that will help you succeed with your networking goals.

Paperback $19.95
eBook $11.95

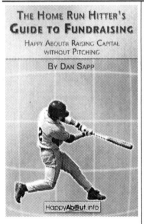

Learn How to Present to Get Funding!

This is a step-by-step guide to help you have the conversation you need to secure the capital you want.

Paperback $19.95
eBook $11.95

Purchase these books at Happy About
http://happyabout.info
or at other online and physical bookstores.

A Message From Super Star Press™

Thank you for your purchase of this 42 Rules Series book. It is available online at http://happyabout.info/42rules/marketing.php or at other online and physical bookstores. To learn more about contributing to books in the 42 Rules series, check out http://42rules.com/write.html

Super Star Press™ is interested in you if you are an author who would like to submit a non-fiction book proposal or a corporation that would like to have a book written for you. Please contact us by e-mail info@superstarpress.com or phone (408-257-3000).

Please contact us for quantity discounts at sales@superstarpress.com

If you want to be informed by e-mail of upcoming books, please e-mail bookupdate@superstarpress.com

Printed in the United States
88164LV00002B/1-99/A